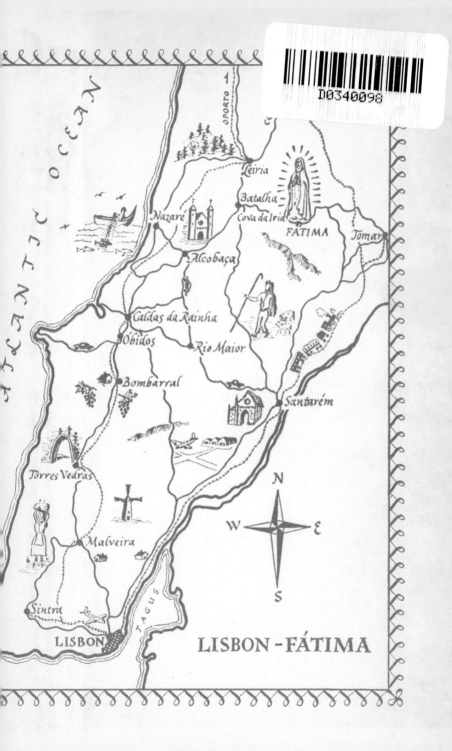

LISBON - FÁTIMA

FÁTIMA:

PILGRIMAGE TO PEACE

FÁTIMA:

PILGRIMAGE TO PEACE

April Oursler Armstrong
and Martin F. Armstrong, Jr.

WITHDRAWN

Hanover House

GARDEN CITY, NEW YORK

NIHIL OBSTAT:

John M. A. Fearns, S.T.D.
Censor Librorum

IMPRIMATUR:

✠ Francis Cardinal Spellman, *Archbishop of New York*

The nihil obstat and imprimatur are official declarations that a book or pamphlet is free of doctrinal or moral error. No implication is contained therein that those who have granted the nihil obstat and imprimatur agree with the contents, opinions, or statements expressed.

New York, May 13, 1954

TO OUR THREE MOTHERS:
GRACE, HENRIETTA, AND

Mary

Acknowledgments

A book is not simply written by one or two people. Its nature, like that of a child, is shaped by men and women near and far, by thoughts and personalities, by concrete help and by dreams. Those who are part of this book's making are far too numerous to mention them all by name, but there are some in particular to whom we cannot refrain from giving public thanks.

When once we had decided to make our pilgrimage, Father James Keller, M.M., founder of the Christophers, introduced us to Father John De Marchi, I.M.C., Superior of the Consolata Order in this country and publisher of *The Rainbow*, a magazine of Fátima mission news. Father De Marchi has lived for years in Fátima and has written one of the finest books available on the history of Fátima, *The Immaculate Heart*. No one

7

could have shared more generously of knowledge and zest for this subject than he.

Foremost among the clergy who aided us, we wish to thank His Eminence, Francis Cardinal Spellman, who armed us with encouragement and his blessing. We wish to thank also Monsignor Umberto Mozzoni, whose enthusiastic support spurred our progress in Portugal. Our thanks also to His Excellency, Bishop Thomas J. McDonnell of Wheeling, West Virginia, for his counsel and guidance.

We are eager to thank especially His Excellency, Bishop José Alves Correia da Silva, of Leiria, and His Excellency, Archbishop Ernesto Sena de Oliveira, of Coimbra, and Canon José Galamba for their extreme kindness in co-operating with us.

The assistance of George Peabody, Jr., added more to our trip than we could ever express. Through his New York and Lisbon offices he supplied us with information and literature and interpreters, and removed for us many of the thorny barriers of international travel and communication. His own personal awareness of the significance of Fátima today in the battle against Communism, his excitement and sense of purpose affected us deeply.

To all at the Consolata Seminário das Missões in Fátima our thanks, in particular to Reverend Aldo Mongiano, Reverend Peter Mongiano, Reverend Francis Maggioni, and Hugh Ferguson. A special note of gratitude to Sister Hyacinth of the Dominican convent in Fátima.

We also wish to thank with briefness necessarily out of all proportion to their contribution to this book:

Ralph Beebe, Miss Frieda Britto, Dr. Jorge Felner da Costa,

Dr. José Manuel da Costa, Charles Cross, Dr. Antonio Figuei-
redo, William B. Glass, Evelyn Hayward, Raymond R. Kohler,
Dr. Ruy Morales de los Rios Leitão, Miss Marion Patton, and
Vincent Goldstein.

Contents

Contents

Chapter One

THE PROMISE OF PEACE

"Why do you, of all people, worry about peace? You know what the prophecies of Our Lady of Fátima say about Russia and about peace, don't you? If you believe them, why aren't you busy praying, and not worrying?"

The healthiest human being can be blind to things he sees every day, like numbers on a telephone dial or the extra notches needed in last year's belt. We had a blind spot about Our Lady of Fátima. A Hollywood movie, a popular song, news stories about some kind of pilgrim statue had passed right by our consciousness. We remembered the Fátima story about the way we remembered nursery rhymes, not too certain of just how it goes or what the point is.

That question from a friend of another faith jolted us into paying attention. "If you believe . . ."

What did we know about the prophecies of Fátima? You could sum it up in one sentence: Mary, the mother of Jesus, appeared to some children in the town of Fátima, Portugal, and asked the world to pray for peace.

We were very vague about Russia's place in the story. We weren't even sure how to pronounce the word "Fátima."

It is pronounced *Fa*-tim-ah. Not Fat-*teem*-ah. Fat-*teem*-ah is the daughter of Mohammed and is also the name of a cigarette and of most exotic dancers in the movies.

Fa-tim-ah is a town in the mountains of Portugal. It is not to be found on any of the standard American maps or atlases. It is not even on most Portuguese maps, but then the people there know where it is without looking it up.

About a hundred families actually live in the parish of Fátima today, but the name has stretched to include a much larger area which was once pasture land and is now a small religious city of seminaries, convents, and hospitals, centered around a new and beautiful church.

Briefly, the significance of Fátima is this: In 1917, in the midst of World War I, when Communism was not a threat but a theory, Our Lady at Fátima made the following prophecies:

1. She foretold the end of World War I.
2. She foretold with precision the time of the outbreaks which would lead to World War II.
3. She foretold the rise of Russia's errors, its annihilation of many nations, and its persecution of all religions.
4. She gave explicit directions for obtaining the conversion of Russia.

5. She gave explicit directions for the establishment of world peace.

If you should enter a Catholic church at the end of Mass, you would see the priest and altar boy kneel on the bottom step and lead the congregation in a series of prayers in English. Everyone in the church knows the purpose of those prayers. They are for the conversion of Russia and for peace in the world. At every single Mass, with the exception of long Solemn High Masses, funerals, and weddings, in every Catholic church across the world those prayers are said each day of the year.

On the first Saturday of any month, if you should pass by a Catholic church, you would see a steady stream of people going to Mass—almost as many as on Sundays. Why?

At Fátima, Our Lady asked for prayer and penance as the only keys to peace. She asked the world to make reparation to God and in particular to receive Holy Communion in the spirit of reparation on the first Saturday of five consecutive months.

Why on the first Saturdays?

The idea was not new with Fátima. As far back as June 13, 1912, Rome had encouraged a devotion of reparation through the Virgin Mary in the form of special prayers to be said on the first Saturday of any month. The time was chosen to avoid conflict with other specific holy days. Five Saturdays may seem a capricious choice, but Our Lady of Fátima was so anxious to encourage this practice that she asked Lucy, now the one surviving child of the three who saw her, to give the world a tremendous promise in her name:

"I promise to assist at the hour of death, with the graces necessary to salvation, all those who on the first Saturday of five consecutive months will go to confession, receive Holy Communion, say the rosary, and keep me company during a quarter of an hour, meditating on the fifteen mysteries of the rosary, with the purpose of making reparation."

And she asked that each person should consecrate himself to her Immaculate Heart. She promised that if the world would cease offending God and would follow her directions, Russia would be converted and peace would return to earth, and her Immaculate Heart would triumph.

What does it mean, the Immaculate Heart?

The standard portrait under that title is enough to make some of the most pious Catholics want to run. Candy-box colors and a simpering smug face, and there stands Mary with a large heart encircled with a ring of thorns. The impression it makes is one of general immodesty and complete betrayal of anatomical science. Popular religious art is in such a lamentable state that even the Pope is officially complaining about it.

Forget the picture, then, for the Immaculate Heart, though of flesh and blood, has given rise to an idea almost impossible to paint or carve. It is a symbol of the love Mary bore the world, and bore to the Son of God, and still harbors for every soul on earth. A love without taint of sin or selfishness, without limits, asking no questions, warming and seeking, and sacrificing.

You cannot show that love in marble or pigment, but you

can find peace through it. That heart is restless with a love that seeks each of God's children. It is that love which led Mary, with God's permission, to appear to three shepherds in Fátima with the message the world is longing to hear—the words of a mother and a Father that can still our fears.

Chapter Two

WHAT REALLY HAPPENED AT FÁTIMA

In the spring of 1916 three children played in the Portuguese hamlet of Aljustrel in the parish of Fátima. Their names were Lucy, Francisco, and Jacinta.

Lucy Santos had just passed her ninth birthday. She was the youngest of seven children. She was dark-haired and olive-skinned, a homely little thing with fierce black eyebrows meeting over her nose. She had two redeeming features, soft glowing eyes and an irrepressible sense of joy.

Lucy was gay and affectionate, annoying her older sisters with her exuberant cuddling. At weddings, at *festas,* or in the small family living room, her feet were impatient to dance. She loved bright clothes, and parties and songs. She loved the solemn stories of saints her mother told, and the tales of elves and giants and magic her father conjured. She loved

God. She made her first Communion at six, an exception made because she knew and understood her catechism so well.

The other two children, brother and sister, were Lucy's cousins, and they lived only a few houses away from her. Francisco was almost eight, a staunch, good-looking lad with a predilection for lizards and flute-playing. Jacinta was six, pert and pretty, and simmering with energy for games and dancing.

Lucy's older sisters were all busy with their own affairs. Two were married; two were working. As the youngest, it became her duty to tend the family's sheep. Her little cousins went with her to the pastures every day, roaming the fields and rocks, idling in the shade of olive trees while the sheep grazed. Days melted into one another in a medley of sunshine and air, music and laughter.

Then came a day different from the rest. They had climbed to the top of a little hill among the olive groves, a miniature craggy peak from which they could see the far-flung mountains of Serra da Aire. The hill was called Cabeço, meaning literally a head, or promontory of rock.

Perched on the stones in the shelter of a weathered tree, they ate their lunch and said their regular noontime rosary as quickly as possible. They played a game with pebbles, a version of "button, button."

Suddenly, in Lucy's own words:

"A strong wind began to shake the trees . . . and then we began to see in the distance, above the trees that stretched to the east, a light whiter than snow, in the form of a young man, quite transparent, and as brilliant as crystal."

He said: "Do not be afraid. I am the Angel of Peace. Pray with me."

They knelt beside him on the bare spot of dirt next to a large white stone and repeated after him a prayer they would never forget:

"My God, I believe, I adore, I hope, and I love You. I ask forgiveness for those who do not believe, nor adore, nor hope, nor love You."

They told no one of the angel's visit. His coming had left them with a strange sense of heaviness and portent. They could not have spoken of him then had they wanted to. In the way of children, they kept their own counsel about the mystery. Alone with their sheep, they prayed daily as he had taught them. And they wondered to themselves.

Summer settled in slow heat over the mountains before the angel came again. This time he surprised them resting in the shade of trees near the well in Lucy's family garden. Gravely he reproved them.

"What are you doing? You must pray! Pray!"

Carefully he explained that by praying and making sacrifices to God they could bring peace to Portugal.

And through the rest of that summer, had anyone chanced to spy, he could have seen three little shepherds, prostrate on the sparse grass of the fields, doing their best to live up to the angel's command.

Then one crisp fall day they pastured their sheep again by the Cabeço. They were kneeling to say the rosary and the angel's prayer. He came again, for the last time.

In his hand he held the Chalice and the Host of Holy

Communion. He left Chalice and Host suspended in mid-air above the white rock and knelt with the children to teach them a new prayer, praising God and begging for the conversion of sinners.

Rising, the angel gave the Host to Lucy and the Chalice to Jacinta and Francisco, saying to them:

"Take and drink the Body and Blood of Jesus Christ, horribly outraged by ungrateful men. Repair their crimes and console your God."

When the angel was gone, they sat imprisoned in silence. They did not want to speak of it, even among themselves. It was as if God had pressed them into secrecy until the proper time.

They had been profoundly shaken. But they were children, after all. Like all youngsters, they did not persist too long in their fine high resolve. They did not forget the angel. But as fall passed into winter, their zeal paled under the other lesser excitements close to hand, the little daily crises of school and home. They slid gently back into their old pattern of casual innocence, and their prayers, once so ardent, were now dispatched to heaven with lighthearted nonchalance. They were quite normal, these three.

The next spring, on Sunday, May 13, 1917, to be exact, they took their sheep to a pasture owned by Lucy's parents some two kilometers away from home. It was a pleasant spot, a rock-strewn natural amphitheater known as the Cova da Iria. It was named after some ancient saint who had lived there, men said, a hermitess named Irene. But Irene and all the saints were far from the children's minds that day of frolicking winds and bright field flowers.

After their picnic lunch they said their rosary in a peculiarly unorthodox manner. Impatient with prayers, they had devised their own shorthand rosary, saying only the first words of each prayer and completely discarding the meditations that properly accompany each decade.

"Our Father, Hail Mary," they chanted. "Hail Mary, Hail Mary . . ."

The whole task was done in two minutes, and they were off to a slope of the Cova to build a house from the rocks that whitened the grass.

Suddenly, from the center of the clear blue sky, two flashes of lightning startled them. As of one accord they looked at the little *azinheira* tree close by them. Just above it, standing on the topmost holly-shaped leaves and acorns, was the figure of a lady about sixteen years old.

The Lady was clothed in light, intense and sparkling and radiant. She herself was as if made of light. She appeared to be wearing a white mantle edged with gold, and she carried a rosary that glistened with inner light. A star seemed to have caught in the folds of her dress. She was surrounded by light, blinding at first, and a little frightening.

Lucy alone was brave enough to address the vision. Simply, matter-of-factly, the Lady said that she had come from heaven. In answer to their question, she said she would tell them exactly who she was on the thirteenth of October. In the meantime, she asked them to return to this same spot on the thirteenth of each of the next five months.

"Will you offer yourselves to God and bear all the sufferings He sends you? In atonement for all the sins that offend Him? And for the conversion of sinners?"

23

"Oh, we will, we will!"

"Then you will have a great deal to suffer, but the grace of God will be with you and will strengthen you. Say the rosary every day to bring peace to the world and an end to war."

With those words the Lady disappeared toward the east, as Lucy says, "in a blaze of light."

What sufferings can children possibly bear to atone for sins? God demands only what each of us can give, and children have their own joys and sorrows, as valiant as older people.

Jacinta could not keep silent about the Lady. With the angel had come a feeling of exhaustion and silence. With the Lady came an overpowering sense of happiness and life. Still, the three children agreed it would be wise to keep their own counsel. They promised each other to say nothing.

Jacinta kept still until after supper. Then she told her mother all about the Lady at the Cova. When her mother did not believe her, she told it again, three times. Jacinta's mother and father, then hearing the same strange tale from Francisco, too, went to Lucy's mother and father and told them. Trouble was born that night.

Lucy's mother, Maria Rosa Santos, was a fine, righteous, devout woman, a female soldier of the Lord. She had an abhorrence of the slightest untruth. And she could not possibly be expected to believe that anyone from heaven was going to come down to talk to her daughter.

Senhora Santos stared at Lucy with horror. Clearly the child was telling a monstrous lie, and a sacrilegious one at that. Senhora Santos took the broomstick out of the corner, and with that and her own saw-toothed tongue she alternately cudgeled and berated her daughter for most of the evening. She got nowhere.

For weeks the distracted mother begged and ordered and demanded that Lucy confess to God and the priest and all the neighbors what a disgraceful liar she was. And Lucy, who loved her mother, could do nothing but simply repeat the facts. Battle raged in the Santos home day after day, until the thirteenth of the next month was upon them.

Now June 13 is the feast day of St. Anthony. And St. Anthony, who, as everyone knows, loves to help people locate lost articles, is, as not everyone knows, a native son of Portugal. You may call him St. Anthony of Padua. But he is also Anthony of Lisbon, and his feast is the greatest of all Portuguese feasts. No child in her right mind would miss the parades and gaiety of that day.

JUNE 13, 1917

Hopefully Senhora Santos dressed Lucy in her finery for the *festa* at Fátima Church. But Lucy did not go to honor St. Antonio. She went, instead, with Francisco and Jacinta to the appointment with the Lady. Their families did not go with them, but they were not alone. Neighbors from Aljustrel and from other towns, too, had heard of the "three seers of Fátima," and they came on foot, with hope and curiosity, to see what would happen at the *azinheira*, or holm-oak tree.

Lightning flashed in the noonday sun, and for the second time the children knelt in the presence of the Lady.

"I want you to continue saying the rosary every day. And

25

after each one of the mysteries, my children, I want you to pray in this way: *'O my Jesus, forgive us and deliver us from the fire of hell. Take all souls to heaven, especially those in greatest need.'* "

"Will you take us to heaven?" asked Lucy.

"Yes. I shall take Jacinta and Francisco soon, but you will remain a little longer, since Jesus wishes you to make me known and loved on earth. He wishes also for you to establish devotion in the world to my Immaculate Heart."

The crowd who knelt around the children did not see the vision. They did see the lightning. As one woman has testified:

"We heard her [Lucy] speak to someone, who, if there at all, was not visible. There was only one mysterious effect to support our impression of another presence there. We heard something like a small, small voice, but could not understand what it was trying to say." And, she continued, when Lucy indicated that Our Lady was leaving, "we saw nothing except a little cloud, a few inches from the tree, which rose very slowly and went backward, toward the east, until we could see it no more."

In that one month the children had become celebrities— most unpopular ones. Strangers and neighbors alike ridiculed and taunted them and questioned them in weary detail. The parents of Jacinta and Francisco, Manuel and Olympia Marto, maintained a tolerant politeness toward their amazing offspring. Lucy's mother and father were outraged at her persistence in "the lie." With the help of the parish priest they almost forced the children to deny it all. So zealous were her mother's attacks that Lucy herself was nearly convinced that she had been deceived by the devil into believing in the Lady. She worried herself into torment, and even decided not to keep the next appointment. Only at the last minute did she change her mind and go to the Cova.

JULY 13, 1917

The story of the Lady of Light had traveled across the rocks to every home in the mountain range. To the shocked surprise of the scoffers of Aljustrel, hundreds of men, women, and children came that day to the Cova da Iria.

The sun was strong, paralyzingly hot. At noon it paled, though the sky remained blue. In the terrible silence that gripped the crowd could be heard "a little buzzing sound." Many said later they had seen a little ball of light settle above the tiny holm oak.

But the sight of the Lady and the sound of her voice were only for the three children.

She repeated her request for the daily rosary "to obtain peace for the world and the end of the war." She again asked them to come each month on the thirteenth, and she promised that in October she would perform a miracle for all to see.

"Make sacrifices for sinners," she said, "and say often, especially while making a sacrifice: *'O Jesus, this is for love of thee, for the conversion of sinners, and in reparation for sins committed against the Immaculate Heart of Mary.'* "

And she told the children a threefold secret, which was soon to cause them severe suffering. Two parts of that secret have now been revealed. The third is still secret.

She opened her hands. In the light between them the children saw a vision of hell, of horror and fiery misery, which terrified them so, that they cried aloud.

The Lady said with sadness: "You have seen hell, where the souls of sinners go. It is to save them that God wants to establish in the world devotion to my Immaculate Heart. If you do what I tell you, many souls will be saved, and there will be peace."

Then followed a prophecy of the fate of men and of nations, of war and of peace from 1917 past the present day, the story of the future we are now living.

With a clap of thunder the vision ended. The mob surged around the children, some with jeers and some with prayers, some trying piously to touch their garments, and others to spit in their solemn little faces and buffet and mock them. Senhor Marto rescued the three of them and carried them home.

For the children life had become a daily horror. Curiosity-seekers tramped at all hours through the low-ceilinged houses of Aljustrel, searching for the tiny seers. Tourists, then as to-day, swarmed over the roads. Lucy's family was in turmoil. To cap all their troubles, the pilgrims had stamped over their gardens, ruining their crops. Their sheep were neglected while the shepherdess answered questions about the Lady. Senhora Santos beat Lucy with the broom handle and called to heaven to witness her daughter's perfidy. Every other woman in the hamlet seemed to deem it her duty to box all three children's ears whenever possible, and to kick at the "heavenly frauds" in passing on the lane.

All of Portugal now knew about the Lady of Fátima. The government, product of a rabidly anti-clerical, atheistic revolutionary movement, was most displeased with the attention these mountain "fairy tales" were attracting. The mayor of the county seat, Arthur Santos (who was proud to be no relation to Lucy Santos), set out to end the hoax which was threatening to disrupt the Republic's suppression of religion.

On August 11 he summoned Lucy, her father, and Senhor Marto to the Town Hall of Ourem. He threatened and cajoled and ordered Lucy to tell him the secret the Lady had confided to her. Lucy stood on her firm ten-year-old legs and quite courteously refused. He promised to kill her if she did not tell him. She still refused. At last he let them all go home.

AUGUST 13, 1917

Without warning, Mayor Santos arrived in Aljustrel. Smilingly he offered to drive the children to the Cova in his own carriage to "protect" them from the crowds. In fact, he insisted they ride with him.

They never reached the Cova. At full speed Mayor Santos carried them to his own house in Vila Nova de Ourem, an hour's trip in the opposite direction. He kept them hidden all day and night in his wife's custody. The next day he called them to his office. With candy and with gold he tried to bribe them. They would not tell the secret.

That afternoon he remanded them to the public jail. They were shoved into a common cell with the county drunkards and thieves. Solemnly the guards assured the children they would not be in prison long. A caldron of oil was being prepared for them. When it boiled they would be brought out to die. In the cell the children wept, and then prayed the rosary.

29

Men who had not seen a church pew in half their lives knelt with them on the dirt floor.

Finally the children stood for the last time before the mayor's desk. He asked Jacinta to choose between dying in oil and telling him the secret. She chose the caldron of oil. Two guards dragged her from the room, and from behind the closed door Francisco and Lucy heard muffled screams.

Francisco was offered the same gambit. He chose death.

Alone, Lucy faced the mayor. She was absolutely convinced, this ten-year-old with the solemn brows, that she was to follow her cousins to a seething death. And she refused to tell the secret or to deny the reality of the vision.

The mayor was defeated. He could do no more. In the morning the children were returned unharmed to their homes.

Meanwhile, on August 13, the Cova held the largest crowd yet seen in those mountains. On foot, by mule and donkey, by bicycle and oxcart, they had come to see the apparitions. Just before noon they learned that the children had been kidnaped by the mayor. Their mutters of anger surged like the sound of an avalanche.

Then a peal of thunder and a flash of lightning silenced them. A delicate white cloud stopped low over the tree, hesitated, then climbed and vanished to the east. Light, strange and many-hued, fell from the sky as from a prism. Trees and earth, rock and the upturned faces of the crowd glowed gold and rose and stained-glass blue.

When it was over, anger had vanished. Quietly the crowds dispersed. And everyone agreed that the Lady had come and gone, without the children.

AUGUST 19, 1917

The children had been home four days. Their ordeal still trembled fresh in their minds. But freedom tasted good, and the children, back at their chores, were almost happy again. They pastured their sheep that afternoon in a stony field called Valinhos, quite near home. Jacinta was not there, only Lucy and Francisco and his brother John.

In the midst of their play, about four o'clock, the sun paled visibly. Lightning flared. Lucy whirled on John and, giving him her only pocket money, wheedled him into fetching Jacinta from home. A few moments after he returned with her, the Lady appeared, this time above another, much larger holm oak, next to a rutted lane.

Calmly, gently, she greeted them, begging them not to let the mayor's mistreatment affright them, and reminding them to come to the Cova on September 13 without fail. She asked them again to say the rosary every day.

And then she was gone.

At the same moment Lucy's older sister, Teresa, was walking homeward with her husband from Moita. Together they saw the sun change color, and the shades of a prism shone on the man's white shirt. It was over in a few minutes. But when she heard what happened at Valinhos, Teresa was not quite so skeptical of her baby sister's tales. Until that time, no one from Lucy's family had yet come to the Cova on the thirteenth.

SEPTEMBER 13, 1917

Thirty thousand pilgrims came to the Cova da Iria, rosaries in their hands and hope stamped on their faces. They saw the darkening of the sun and the globe of light above the miniature tree.

Once more, for the children's ears alone, the Lady repeated her pleas for prayer that war might end.

Said Lucy, "So many believe that I am an impostor and a cheat that they say I deserve to be hanged and burned. Will you please perform a miracle so that all of them can believe?"

The Lady promised.

When she was gone, the children, guileless and smiling, announced to everyone that precisely at noon on October 13 a great miracle would occur—one that everyone could see and believe. A tremendous risk for hoaxters to take, categorically naming the date and the hour!

They were the only people in the world who had no fears about that prediction. But then, they knew where it came from.

Already the Portuguese Government was openly planning the removal of these three diminutive subversives; October 13 seemed a handmade opportunity. The newspapers chortled with satirical glee. They ran a series scheduled to climax on October 13, pitched to the failure of the miracle. Various Freemason organizations and civic groups threatened to bomb the children's homes.

As the first leaves of October fell, Lucy's parents were close to panic. Again and again her harassed mother would shake Lucy out of midnight slumber, imploring her to confess all before it was too late.

OCTOBER 13, 1917

Rain, relentless and cold, had set in the night before. The hard red clay of the roads turned to sludge. Sight-seers jammed the Marto house, clambering with muddy feet on chairs and beds to gawk as Jacinta and Francisco dressed. When Lucy joined them to walk to the Cova they could hardly move through the throngs.

A bitter wind swept down from the northwest. The rain seemed to be specially sent to erase all thoughts of heaven and shining white ladies. Seventy thousand people, who had traveled for days from all over Portugal, stood patiently under stolid black umbrellas. As the morning grew old, the rain grew fiercer. It could not silence the voices praying the rosary, nor the hymns ringing out over the dismal mountain range.

Exactly at noon, Standard Time, the children fell to their knees in the mud. Rain dripped from their upturned chins. The Lady had come.

"I want a chapel built here in my honor. I want you to continue saying the rosary every day.

"The war will end within a year, and the soldiers will return to their homes. . . ."

"Yes," said Lucy. And remembering the promise made in May, she asked, "Will you tell me your name?"

"I am the Lady of the Rosary."

And a little later: "People must amend their lives, and ask

33

pardon for their sins. They must not offend Our Lord any more, for He is already too much offended!"

Before the children's eyes, Our Lady of the Rosary rose slowly toward the dark heavens. And to them was given a vision of paradise. They saw her in a mantle of blue, and beside her St. Joseph with the Christ Child in his arms. St. Joseph, all in white, leaned from the clouds and three times blessed the earth. And then he was gone, and in the pale sun stood Christ Himself, tall in His red cloak, and beside Him, Mary in the traditional garb of Our Lady of Sorrows. Solemnly, lovingly, Christ blessed the people below. And as that vision passed, Lucy alone saw Mary poised for an instant in the figure of Our Lady of Mount Carmel.

But the miracle? The people in the Cova did not see those visions. Instead, at the instant of the vision they heard Lucy cry:

"Look at the sun!"

Instantaneously the rain stopped. The black clouds split asunder, racing to the corners of the sky. The sun alone stood in the heavens, a sun such as man has never seen before. Without blinking, the throngs could stare directly into it. It was the color of mother-of-pearl. Yet there was neither mist nor cloud to dim it.

The sun in the noonday sky began to tremble and spin, whirling in a frenzy of fire. From it spun a thousand colors, red and blue, green and yellow, and the infinite shades between. It turned on itself, thrilling and twisting, dancing in the sky.

For a moment it paused in balance. Then, as if the bonds of nature were loosed, as if the universe were split apart, it

34

seemed to plummet to earth. Heat and destruction hurtled downward, driving people to their knees.

At the last possible second the sun retreated. The sky settled. Men blinked and turned away from the blinding rays. It was noon in a brilliant sheep pasture in the mountains of Portugal. The ground, the grass, the clothes of the crowd, even their hair, were dry.

That, in necessarily inadequate words, was the miracle of the sun.

Did it really happen? Every one of the seventy thousand who were there that day swore they saw it. Many are living now to testify to it. People many kilometers away, even some who through illness or monastic seclusion had not heard of the promise and did not expect anything unusual, reported they saw the sun dance.

Among the witnesses, two are especially interesting. One is a university professor from Coimbra, Dr. Almeida Garett, a learned man not given to believing or spreading idle tales.

Dr. Garett confesses that the morning's rain had tried his patience almost beyond endurance. Even when Lucy cried out, he says, he looked at the sky "with diminishing curiosity because a long time had passed without anything to excite me." The sun, he remembers, "looked like a glazed wheel. . . . It could not be confused with the sun seen through fog (for there was no fog . . .) because it was not opaque. . . . It was a remarkable fact that one could fix one's eyes on this brazier of heat and light without any pain . . . or blinding of the retina.

"This was not the sparkling of a heavenly body, for it spun around on itself in a mad whirl. Then, suddenly, one heard a clamor, a cry of anguish breaking from all the people. The sun, whirling wildly, seemed to loosen itself from the firmament and advance threateningly upon the earth as if to crush us with its huge and fiery weight."

An even more valuable report appeared in the pro-government newspaper, O Seculo. It was written by an avowed scoffer, Avelino de Almeida. Senhor Almeida had been specifically assigned to cover the "Fraud of Fátima." For months this able journalist had been poking arrogant, intellectual fun at the mountain miracles. He had awaited October 13 as the crowning opportunity for his satirical skill.

No trace of humor mars his careful eyewitness report, published on the front page the next morning.

"From the road . . . one could see the immense multitude turn toward the sun. . . . It looked like a plaque of dull silver, and it was possible to look at it without the least discomfort. It might have been an eclipse which was taking place. But at that moment a great shout went up and one could hear the spectators nearest at hand shouting: 'A miracle!'

"Before the astonished eyes of the crowd, whose aspect was biblical as they stood bareheaded, eagerly searching the sky, the sun trembled, made sudden incredible movements outside all cosmic laws—the sun 'danced,' according to the typical expression of the people."

The phenomenon of the sun was seen by seventy thousand people of every type, scoffers and devout alike, and was seen by disinterested observers miles away. Therefore, it could not have been due to mass hypnosis, nor a group delusion.

The phenomenon of the sun was not noted at any astronomical observatory. By the measurements of science it could not—and did not—happen. Therefore, it could not have been natural in origin.

It occurred at the precise moment that the children had predicted a month beforehand.

Given those facts, it is at least easy for a reasonable person to understand why millions of people of all faiths believe, as we do, that the whirling of the sun was indeed the miracle the Lady had promised, "the miracle that would enable all to believe."

Chapter Three

SECRETS OF THE FUTURE

There is smug satisfaction in testing any prophecy, even an almanac's weather predictions. Let a soothsayer veil his reports in symbolism, redolent of mystic numbers and nightmare gargoyles, and the dullest mind is tempted into supernatural sleuthing.

History is peopled with dramatic seers—with Cassandra and Nostradamus, the witch of Endor and the hanky-panky mouthings of unnaturally blond women who claim to talk with ghosts. Among the frauds stand a few God-chosen sayers of truth—the bearded Isaias and the gaunt figure of John the Baptist crying in the wilderness.

But the prophets of Fátima are different. They are children who could not read or write, who had never traveled as far as the seaside town of Nazaré some thirty miles away. They knew nothing of world affairs. They could only repeat what was told them by Our Lady of the Rosary. And they spoke not in symbols, but in definite terms.

What actually did they foretell?

The Lady of the vision, in 1917, confided to them a secret in three parts.

The first part was a vision of hell, a terrifying picture of the results of sin. It was to remind the world of that discarded concept of sin—not neurosis, or maladjustment, or environmental difficulties, but sin—that Our Lady had come down from heaven. And in terms the children could understand she revealed in the light between her outstretched hands "a sea of fire. Plunged in this flame were devils and souls . . . ; these were suspended in flames which seemed to come from the forms themselves—there to remain, without weight or equilibrium, amid cries of pain and despair which horrified us so that we trembled with fear." That is Lucy's own testimony of the vision, taken from her memoirs.

Hell is an unfashionable thought these days. Fire and brimstone went out with ankle-length dresses and high collars. But fashion is passing, and hell is eternal. And the Lady from heaven came to remind us that sin is real and that those who offend God will not only suffer on this earth but will burn with a fire from within, in self-made torment, in the next world.

And as Lucy herself has quoted the prophecies, this is what the Lady of the Rosary told the children on July 13, 1917:

"You have seen hell, where the souls of sinners go. It is to save them that God wants to establish in the world devotion to my Immaculate Heart. If you do what I tell you, many souls will be saved, and there will be peace. This war will end, but if men do not refrain from offending God, another and more terrible war will begin."

How definite was the prediction of the next war, which we now call World War II?

In the same place in her memoirs, Lucy testifies that Our Lady mentioned that the next war would occur in the pontificate of Pope Pius XI, specifically mentioning his name. At the time of the prophecy the Pope was Benedict XV. There was no way for human beings to determine the name of his successor.

In addition, little Jacinta later told her friends in Lisbon, in the year 1918: "If men do not amend their lives, Our Lady will send the world a punishment worse than anything it has known before, and it will come first to Spain."

And continuing with Lucy's report of the prophecies made on July 13, 1917, we read that Our Lady said:

"When you see a night that is lit by a strange and unknown light, you will know it is the sign God gives you that He is about to punish the world with war and with hunger, and by the persecution of the Church and the Holy Father.

"To prevent this, I shall come to the world to ask that Russia be consecrated to my Immaculate Heart, and I shall ask that on the first Saturday of every month Communions of reparation be made in atonement for the sins of the world.

"If my wishes are fulfilled, Russia will be converted and there will be peace. If not, then Russia will spread her errors throughout the world, bringing new wars and persecution of the Church. The good will be martyred, and the Holy Father will have much to suffer. Certain nations will be annihilated.

"But in the end my Immaculate Heart will triumph. The

Holy Father will consecrate Russia to me, and she will be converted, and the world will enjoy a period of peace.

"In Portugal the Dogma of Faith will always be preserved."

In 1917 the "war to end wars" was at its height, yet Our Lady foretold the coming of World War II. Russia was then still known as a prominent Christian stronghold, and Lenin had only a few months before crossed its borders in the sealed car, yet Our Lady foretold the rise of Russia's errors and her need for conversion years later. Portugal was in the grip of a militantly atheistic government and her churches firmly oppressed, yet she said that the faith would always survive in that land.

Those are predictions that can be tested, as the prophecy of hell cannot. They were part of the secret the Lady of the Rosary confided to three children in a rocky pasture of Portugal —the prediction of the wars and persecutions that we are now witnessing, and of the one and only remedy for them, the key to peace.

Refrain from offending God. Atone for the sins of the world. Recognize sin for what it really is. Pray—and repent.

The children did not immediately reveal their secret. Our Lady had forbidden them to tell it to anyone until she gave them permission. The mayor with his bribes and his boiling oil had failed. Their parents failed. Priests badgered them. Rich and poor alike offered them presents to hear the secret. The children did not tell.

And why not, when the message was of such devastating

importance? Because the Lady had forbidden them. Their own natural desire for importance could not transcend that.

A year after the October apparition, Francisco and Jacinta fell victim to a virulent epidemic of influenza.

One afternoon Our Lady appeared to them again as they lay in their plain wooden beds. She said that she would take Francisco to heaven very soon, an announcement that made the boy very happy. After a brief glimpse of heaven's glory, he felt like a stranger on earth.

Then she asked Jacinta if the girl would be willing to convert more sinners. Jacinta agreed with enthusiastic wide eyes. Our Lady explained to her that she would have to go to two hospitals, and suffer for many months, to make further sacrifices, and to atone for the sins of the world. And then, said Our Lady, Jacinta would die, away from home and quite bereft of family or friends. The idea of that loneliness frightened the child, but her eyes were fixed on heaven, and she was eager to do as much as she could to serve Our Lord. She could have refused. She did not.

Six months later, on April 4, 1919, after receiving his First Communion in his sickbed in the tiny bedroom of the Marto house, Francisco died, smiling, at the age of eleven. He had never been too clever at remembering his catechism, and that was why the parish priest had never judged him worthy of Communion earlier.

Jacinta uncomplainingly progressed from influenza to bronchial pneumonia and pleurisy, with a painful abscess in her chest. In the summer she was sent to a hospital in Vila

43

Nova de Ourem, but the open wound in her side could not be healed. She returned home with tuberculosis.

That December, Our Lady came again, and explained to Jacinta that she would be taken to a hospital in Lisbon, never again to see Lucy or her own family. She would soon die, in Lisbon.

Her family meant to keep her at home, but they were over-ridden. At the insistence of a group of doctors and priests who feared that the Martos would believe the child's tale of going to heaven so soon and therefore would neglect to give her proper care, Jacinta was indeed sent to Lisbon. She was first housed at an orphanage and finally in a ward of the Estafania Hospital. She was in deep pain, but she remained extraordinarily cheerful. She also astounded those around her with certain short-term prophecies, readily verified. She read the souls of her doctors and nurses and begged them to mend their ways. And the tragedies of which she spoke came to pass.

On February 10, 1920, an operation was performed, removing two tubercular ribs from her left side, leaving a hole the size of a man's hand. Our Lady appeared again to her and promised, as Jacinta reported, "that she would come to take me almost right away." From that moment on her pain vanished. On February 20 she died, at the age of ten. Only a nurse, a stranger, was at her side. She did not receive Holy Viaticum. The priest who was to bring her Communion decided he had time to wait till morning.

As for Lucy, at the insistence of the Bishop of Leiria, whose newly restored diocese embraced Fátima, she was hidden away in a convent school the very next year. In 1925, at the age of nineteen, she entered the novitiate of the Dorothean nuns in

Spain (Portuguese convents were almost nonexistent under the laws of the Republic). She lived in complete enforced obscurity for many years, even being given another name. No mention of Fátima or of the growing devotions at the shrine was permitted in her presence. The Bishop, in his wisdom, felt that in all charity she should be relieved of the daily questions and petitions of thousands of investigators and sight-seers which she had endured for four years at home after the apparitions. Also, since the Church had not yet reached any official decision about the truth of the apparitions, the Bishop prudently removed the one remaining "seer," in order to discover whether the crowds would diminish after Lucy was no longer on view.

Obediently Lucy went about her appointed tasks, keeping her heavenly secret to herself. Then, in the first year of her novitiate, on December 10, 1925, Our Lady appeared to her in her cell and said:

"Look, my daughter, at my Heart . . . which ungrateful men pierce at every moment with their blasphemy and ingratitude. You, at least, try to console me with the practice of the first Saturdays."

From that moment on Lucy did her best to urge those around her and those she could reach by letter to receive Communion on the first Saturday of five consecutive months in reparation to the Immaculate Heart, along with the making of a good confession, the praying of the rosary, and a fifteen-minute devotion on the mysteries of the rosary. But it was far from a widespread crusade.

Then in 1929, in the Dorothean chapel in Túy, Spain, Our Lady came again to ask for the consecration of Russia by the

Holy Father in union with all the bishops of the world. Through her confessor and the Bishop of Leiria, Lucy managed to send this message to Pope Pius XI. Nothing whatsoever was done about it, probably because no great leader of a state or of a church is predisposed to take orders from a twenty-one-year-old nun from the backwoods of Portugal.

But the Church was not ignoring Fátima. The Bishop of Leiria was conducting intensive investigations of the truth of the apparitions. His committees, made up chiefly of men who did not immediately believe in the children's tale, interviewed every surviving witness, including Lucy. They examined the hundreds of cases of alleged miracles. For years they worked, resolved that no chicanery could deceive them. Year by year, in spite of all official discouragement, the number of pilgrims grew. In October 1930, thirteen years after the secret, the Bishop was fully satisfied of the truth, as reported by the commissions. He gave official approval to the cult of Our Lady of Fátima and declared the visions of the shepherd children worthy of belief.

Lucy, by then a full-fledged Dorothean nun, endured all the terrible years of the thirties, watching in enforced silence as the dreaded war came ever nearer.

Civil War struck in Spain, the first formidable contest with Communism in the European world. The bishops of Portugal, in 1936, only a few miles from the bloodshed and destruction in their sister country of Spain, implored the protection of the Blessed Virgin against war and Communism and made a vow of a thanksgiving pilgrimage two years later if they were spared. Portugal stood untouched throughout the conflict, and in 1938 the pilgrimage was made.

On January 24 and 25, 1938, the most startling and brilliant aurora borealis ever seen seared the skies of Europe. So terrifying were the lights that newspapers all over the world commented on them, and many speculated on their meaning. Lucy saw those strange, twisting illuminations in the midnight sky and fell to her knees in prayer.

"And when you see a night that is lit by a strange and unknown light," Our Lady had said, "you will know it is the sign given that He is about to punish the world with war. . . ."

"In the pontificate of Pius XI," said Lucy.

Lucy knew that the light was an aurora borealis, of natural origin. But to her it had a preternatural meaning. She redoubled her efforts to convey the message of Our Lady to Pius XI and to all those in authority. But on the night of March 11, 1938, Hitler's troops marched into Austria. War was not declared, but it had begun.

Almost one year later to the day, the Catholic Church had a new Pope, Eugene Pacelli, called Pius XII. This was the Pope who was to become famous as the opponent of Communism and the devotee of Our Lady. To him, on the orders of her spiritual directors, Lucy wrote, explaining again that Our Lady had asked the consecration of Russia. And Pope Pius XII heeded her request.

In October 1942, when most of the world was still praising Russia as a magnanimous ally, in the fourth year of the second and more terrible war which had come as Our Lady had predicted, Pius XII consecrated the whole world, with special mention of Russia, to the Immaculate Heart. Ten years later, in July 1952, he publicly made a special consecration of "all

47

peoples of Russia . . . in confident assurance that [we may obtain] true peace."

Lucy's secret at last was open to the public.

But why on earth, or under heaven, did Lucy wait so long to reveal so important a prophecy? Part of the delay was not of her making; the responsibility for it lies on the prudently slow workings of a gigantic organization that is human as well as inspired. Still, Our Lady told Lucy about Russia in 1917, and Lucy did not even try to make the prophecy public until 1929. For a prophecy to be dramatic, it must come well in advance of the event. Such bad timing leaves Lucy open to the most cynical sneers. To the incredulous it seems to destroy the value of every word she says!

Lucy knows that.

"It may seem that I should have revealed these things sooner than I did, and that their value would have been doubled," she says. "It might have been so if God had wished me to appear before the world as a prophetess, but such was not His Will. If it had been, He would not have ordered me to keep silence, but to speak. I think Our Lady only wished to make use of me to remind the world of the need to avoid sin, and of reparation by prayer and penance for so many offenses against God."

There is no answer to that.

Lucy remained a Dorothean sister, accessible to all who had good reason to visit her, until May 13, 1948. That month, for the first time, she revisited her home and saw the shrine that now stood where once Our Lady had stood. Then, on the thirty-first anniversary of the apparition, she was at last granted her life's wish. She entered the Carmelite Order. She lives today in a convent in the ancient Portuguese university town of Coimbra, almost completely isolated from the world. She spends her days in prayer and meditation.

One part of her secret is still to be revealed. One prophecy, dating from 1917, is still locked in tantalizing silence.

We had heard many stories about this third secret, some quite appalling. We had heard from credible sources that the Holy Father had read it and had fallen sobbing to his knees. We had heard from equally reliable lips that no one in the world had read it. Some said it contained the date of the end of the world. Others said with round-eyed solemnity that it dealt with the coming of the Anti-Christ. We had heard speculations that, when opened, it would be found to deal with events that had already happened.

Everyone agreed that the secret was in the keeping of the Bishop of Leiria and absolutely could not be opened until 1960. But a news story in a most unsensational paper asserted that though it could not be opened before that date, there was no guarantee, no binding reason, why its revelations could not then be postponed till a much later date.

Being secret-lovers ourselves, we resolved to do our utmost to learn the truth about that last secret once we reached Portugal.

Because already, almost without realizing it, we had decided we must go to Fátima ourselves in search of peace.

Chapter Four

PILGRIMS IN LISBON

Chaucer would have despaired of us. No horses. No callused feet. No overnight stops at a wayside inn. We made our pilgrimage by air.

We went to Portugal by TWA. We left New York at eight o'clock at night, and fourteen hours later we were in Lisbon. Our watches still ran on New York time, but the world had been spinning beneath us. En route the sun came up to dazzle us at three in the morning, our time, and at six we made our one stop, on the tiny wave-swept islands of the Azores. Already in Portuguese territory, we tasted fresh passionfruit juice and native pineapples for breakfast. The next land we saw was Portugal. It was ten in the morning back in New York, but in Lisbon the bells were chiming three.

In little more than half a day we had come to another world.

Lisbon is a city without equal for charm. She is like an oriental beauty, trained to offer continually new delights to her suitors, wise and lovely, kind and unassuming.

Like Rome, Lisbon is built on seven hills. Like Paris, her byways are colorful with sidewalk cafés, golden with sun. Some of her side streets, steep-stepped with cobblestones, too narrow for an automobile, whisper of the days when the Moors ruled this land. But her housing projects are as efficient as the newest American ones, and they wear red-tiled roofs and door pieces of the Madonna in blue-and-white tile. Lisbon is a city of color, of avenues set with meticulously carved gardens of scarlet cannas and blinding marigolds, of hedges and stately palms.

We had two days in Lisbon before our trip to Fátima, two days to learn what Portugal was all about. We rocketed around the city in busses and cable cars. We rode the famous elevator, built by Monsieur Eiffel about the same time as the Paris Tower. So steep are the hills that this giant outdoor machine is constantly in use, carrying pedestrians from one main street in a valley business district to the parallel street on the hilltop. The ride costs about a penny and is used by Lisbonese as casually as a subway or a bus. The view from the top landing is dizzy and gorgeous, stretching over the whole city down to the mighty Tagus River and the Atlantic.

But Lisbon is a city not only for sight-seers, but for the devout as well. Hundreds of churches, varying in style from the sharp-lined modernity of Nossa Senhora da Fátima to the mosaics and lapis lazuli pillars of the Renaissance São Roque, stand in eloquent testimony to the faith that is as much a part of Portugal as her mellow sunlight. On the heights of Lisbon the white dome and twin towers of the Estrella glisten like a beacon, to be seen for miles along the Tagus.

Portugal was born Catholic, a daughter of Our Lady. In the battle of Aljubarrota in 1385, eleven hundred Portuguese routed thirty thousand Spaniards to gain their freedom from the kingdom of León. That independence, the true beginning of Portugal, was won by John I, who carried a banner with the figure of the Blessed Virgin into the fray. In gratitude he built the nation's first monument, the exquisite cathedral of Our Lady of Victory at Batalha.

The Crusaders had camped in Lisbon as early as the twelfth century. With their help the Portuguese under Our Lady drove the Moslem Moors out of the land after six centuries of conquest and brutal oppression. On the peak of the Alfama, the old quarter of Lisbon, stand the Castle of St. George and the ruins of the ancient Moorish fortress.

From that romantic and storied spot we wandered down into the heart of the old city to the Cathedral, or Sé, once the chief place of prayer for the Crusaders. Founded in 1150, it has survived two major earthquakes, to preserve the tomb of Lisbon's patron saint, St. Vincent, who settled on this spot in the third century. The coat of arms of Lisbon, bearing a ship and two ravens, recalls the ancient legend of the birds who led the saint to harbor on the shores of the Tagus. As we stood in the Cathedral, with black-shawled women murmuring prayers to the Virgin where once knights in armor knelt, the past seemed to merge with the present in the shadows beyond the votive candlelight.

The Sé was less than fifty years old when a young Portuguese mother carried a son to be baptized at the font. She

called him Ferdinand. He was educated in this cathedral
school and sang in this choir long before the world learned to
call him St. Anthony of Padua. On the stairs leading to the
choir, so the story goes, the devil once appeared to him in the
form of a beautiful woman, tempting him to sin. Anthony, in
self-protection, traced the sign of the cross with his finger on
the stone wall of the stairs. The devil vanished, but the cross
remained as if carved into the rock. We saw it there, painted
over with gold, halfway up those steps worn and rounded by
centuries of reverent feet.

Not far away is the simple little Franciscan church which
marks the exact spot of St. Anthony's birth. Trailing a brown-
robed friar down the winding stairs below the street level, we
stood before the bare stone alcove where the patron of all lost
things, and of the poor, and of pregnant women, was born
more than seven hundred and fifty years before. A shipwreck
later cast him on the shores of Italy, but no accident can steal
him from the heart of Portugal. And as the friar reminded us,
"St. Anthony was devoted to Our Lady, too, you know. He
once had a vision of her Son, the Infant Jesus. He knew Our
Lady well."

From the twelfth-century aura of the Alfama we drove
through the newer part of Lisbon, past the handsome Praça do
Comércio, or Black Horse Square, westward along the Tagus
to Belém—straight into the heart of the fifteenth and sixteenth
centuries, the years when Portugal vanquished the terrors of
the seven seas.

On the river front stands a small fortress, the Tôrre de
Belém, or Tower of Bethlehem, built in 1520 to honor the
ocean explorers of this land. On this spot the great navigators

had knelt to implore the blessings of Our Lady, Queen of the Sea, before venturing into the unknown. Here Bartholomew Diaz knelt before the voyage that rounded the Cape of Good Hope. Vasco da Gama prayed here as he left for the fabled land of India. From Belém sailed Lourenço Marques to discover Madagascar, and Cabral to discover Brazil. Even in these years, Portuguese sailors still come to Belém to ask Our Lady's protection before embarking for the fishing banks of Newfoundland.

Across the road stands the magnificent Convento dos Jeronymos, raised in 1499 to commemorate Vasco da Gama's discovery of the sea route to India. In that high-vaulted church the explorer lies buried, and the fifteenth-century statue of Our Lady which he venerated still stands, not far from the newer, beautiful statue of Our Lady of Fátima.

A few doors down the street is the royal Ajuda palace, named after Nossa Senhora de Ajuda, Our Lady of Aid. Within its musty walls stands the world's finest collection of state coaches. We wandered a few moments among those mammoth gilt vehicles, between rows of cabriolets and sedan chairs, down aisles of coaches specially designed for little princes, and for royal brides, and for aging envoys, mute evidence of glory that has passed forever.

There is no throne in Portugal today. The kings who swore allegiance to Our Lady, who dreamed of opening the shores of distant seas to her gentle sway, are gone, victims of their own self-will. By the turn of this century the people had grown weary of incompetent rule. Portugal's treasury was nearly empty. In October 1910, revolution struck.

The rebels agreed on two things: that they hated the mon-

55

archists and feared and loathed the Roman Catholic Church. They disestablished the Church, expelled all religious orders, and abolished the teaching of religion in the schools. Beyond that they could not agree. Turmoil ruled the avenues of Lisbon, and blood was shed from Belém to Oporto. Twenty-four separate revolutions erupted in the next seventeen years as faction battled faction. In 1921 the founder of the Republic was murdered. By 1926 forty cabinets had come and gone. The currency was valueless. Portugal was in her death throes.

Two generals marched into Lisbon and took command. From his desk at the University of Coimbra they summoned a young professor of political economy, a man already known for his cool governmental head, Dr. Antonio de Oliveira Salazar. They appointed him Minister of Finance. He stayed five days, then left in disgust because he had been given full responsibility and no authority.

Two years later the whole country was begging Salazar to return. He did, receiving complete authority over national finance. In little more than a year he balanced the budget. He redeemed all foreign loans and made Portugal completely self-supporting. To this day the escudo ranks with the Swiss franc as the soundest currency in the world.

Four years later Salazar became Prime Minister and founded what is known as the "New State," with a president and a National Assembly, a hybrid between an authoritarian state and a democracy. He built roads and schools, hospitals, power stations and dams. He rebuilt the economy of the nation. Out of anarchy he brought order, combining the natural desire for liberty with the slow advance toward political education that is necessary after centuries of complete monarchy. There is only one party in Portugal. A few years ago Salazar tried to enlist the leaders necessary to start an opposition, but the attempt fell through. Salazar has brought complete internal peace and freedom from war. He governs the third largest empire in the world, with colonies in Africa, Asia, and Oceania, with no unrest.

But he had done more. To the land of Our Lady, Salazar has restored freedom to the faith of centuries. He has returned religion to the classroom and priests to their altars. He is deeply religious himself. For five years he studied at a seminary before going to Coimbra. At the university for nearly twenty years he roomed with a student priest who is now Cardinal of Lisbon.

We drove past his residence at the former monastery of Santo Bento, now the Palace of Parliament, where he lives with his adopted daughters. He has never married. His life is as bare of luxuries as a monk's. He lives to serve Portugal and his God. He still hopes to return to Coimbra to his studies. By his own request he has been listed in the university catalogue as "professor on leave" for the past twenty-six years.

Salazar was not in Lisbon when we arrived. He was away on retreat, in that silence of prayer and self-evaluation which nourishes the soul.

Already in our first day we had come to understand why Portugal was truly Our Lady's land. But we had yet to come to know her people, the people entrusted with the message of Fátima.

Like so many Americans, we had made the mistake of believing that Portugal was practically the same as Spain. It is as different as the United States is from Mexico. The language, the customs, the inborn spirit of Portugal are unique, and its history and culture superbly individual. The people of Portugal are like no others in the world, yet in their own way they combine the best that is in all of us. To know them is to know in part what is meant by the children of God.

They are gay as children are gay, wisely careless of time. They are never too hurried to be kind or to enjoy the blessing of a moment's sunshine or an hour's desultory talk. They work hard and earnestly, but not long. They take their amusements very seriously.

We followed a jaunty thronging crowd to the Campo Pequeno to witness a bullfight. In the large semi-Moorish arena the air sparkled on the scarlet and yellow and white shawls hung from every box seat. Flowers pelted the matadors, and cruelty was absent from the ring. In Portugal the bull is never killed in the fight and men are truly brave.

Through an amber sunset we walked from the gaiety of the arena to the somber back streets, away from the glitter of neon-lit movie houses and the shouts of lottery-ticket sellers. We went to listen to the native sound of Lisbon, to the *"fado singers"*—soulful-eyed women in black shawls, chanting songs of fate. Their words are mournful, sad as life is sad, but their music lilts through the night air, refusing to bow under the weight of tragedy.

Through the moonlight we drove to our hotel in Estoril, seaside suburb of Lisbon, the Riviera of Portugal. Here ex-kings live on thin purses, with the lights of the gambling casino at their backs and the endless white breakers and sand at their feet. Just beyond loomed the enchanted mountains of Sintra, where Lord Byron had once pursued beauty and where the fairy-tale palaces of the rulers of Portugal still beckon the dreamer.

A bull ring, a *fado* club, a resort of kings old and new—strange beginning for a pilgrimage. But in that night we caught a bit more of the spirit of this land Our Lady chose.

It was part of the puzzle of Fátima.

Chapter Five

THE TOWN OF THE BAKER'S WIFE

It is roughly a hundred miles from Lisbon to Fátima.

Our road led north through vineyards and olive groves, through the broad fields, the *lezirias*, past tall stands of cork trees and wide-walled *quintas*, or farms. Through the bull-breeding farms of Vila Franca de Xira we drove, turning north-west along a fine highway to skirt the charming thirteenth-century town of Óbidos. Rice paddies startled us as we drove under the whirling shadows of staunch sunbaked windmills into Caldas da Rainha, a popular spa whose name means literally Hot Springs of the Queen. We stretched our legs in the square, peering into the famous pottery and porcelain factories, and pausing to buy some of the rock-like sugar buns for which the town is known. We found them interesting and inedible, but our bagful made friends for life out of all the children we were to meet in the next few days.

On we went northeast to the city of Alcobaça, home of the memory-strewn twelfth-century monastery of Santa Maria. The largest in Portugal, this once housed close to a thousand Cistercians. Today it is a government home for old men, and the church adjoining it is preserved as a national monument of faith. Aside from all history, Santa Maria is remarkable for one feature—its kitchen.

The size of four small-family houses, it is all tiled in delicate blue, trimmed with massive dark beams, and equipped with tables and fireplaces scaled to butcher and cook several oxen at once. And a river, the Alco, runs directly under those fireplaces, surfacing inside the kitchen.

These wily monks, eight hundred years ago, straddled their built-in stream with a large tank at the far end of the room. The clear water poured into the tank, depositing an ample number of glistening fresh fish to be detained until dinnertime. The stream itself continues on into the open air, obediently removing all waste. Running water, refrigeration, and garbage disposal, still in working order to this day!

In the church itself is the solemn Sala dos Reis, the room where the kings of Portugal traditionally received their crowns. Here, too, are the tombs of the first king of Portugal and many other rulers, including the infamous King Pedro the Cruel and his mistress, Inés de Castro. As we left Santa Maria the guide nudged Martin and said:

"Did you notice that the tombs of Pedro and his woman are placed not side by side but foot to foot?"

Martin nodded.

"The King ordered it just that way, so that when they rise from their graves on Judgment Day the first thing they will see will be each other." The guide grinned. "A foresighted man, King Pedro."

From Alcobaça we made a short detour to the most colorful town in Portugal, the fishing village of Nazaré, named for the home town of the Lord.

The people of Nazaré are quite unlike their neighbors. They claim to be of pure Phoenician descent. Darker in skin, these men of the sea still fish from craft with carved prows and strange eyes painted on the bows. Back in the days when the Duke of Wellington battled Napoleon, so the story goes, a Scotch ship was wrecked on the treacherous sand bars of Nazaré Harbor. The townsfolk caught their first glimpse of a tartan. Plaid hypnotized them, but the Scotch greens and reds seemed a little prosaic to the Nazarenes. They fell to weaving their own, in pink and yellow and pale green, orange and purple, azure and coral and black. They cling to them still. The one rule of fashion on that sandy stretch of coast is that the plaid of a shirt must never match the plaid of the trousers or skirt with which it is worn. And the patches must match nothing at all.

The beach is broad and beautiful, strewn with nets drying in the sun, and fishermen coiling and knotting their ropes beside their flamboyant boats. Children skitter through the sand, browned and laughing, hiding behind pigskins full of fresh water, or under the sails stretched out for mending. Nazaré is a haven of color and joy when the fishermen are home.

The harbor lies at the foot of a startling steep cliff, jagged against the cloudless sky. It was to see that cliff that we had come to Nazaré.

Legend tells us that in the fifteenth century the duke of

63

this countryside went hunting on his fine white steed in chase
of a noble stag. The stag, slow to capture, ran at full speed
toward the edge of this cliff and plummeted to death, four
hundred feet to the sea. The duke was at the edge of the
precipice. Suddenly the Virgin Mary herself, to whom the
duke had always turned in joy and in need, appeared and
halted the horse in its tracks. The duke was saved, and his
people and their descendants have cherished devotion to the
Virgin under their own special title, Our Lady of Nazaré.

Someone had suggested that the children of Fátima, who
had certainly heard of this "apparition" and seen pictures of
the statue, might have used it as a basis to create their own
new legend. We stood at the top of the cliff where the rock
juts out like a bowsprit over ocean, and wondered. The Lady
of Nazaré was a purely local outgrowth; she came with no
message, and the world has still not heard of her, as it has
heard of Fátima.

We entered the tiny square whitewashed shrine on the peak
and stared at the statue of this apparition. We saw a short,
plump, gaudily dressed little figure with a fatuous smile. There
was no resemblance here to the slender young Lady in white,
whose face was gentle, but sad, and whose words were to
alter the history of our world.

The drying nets and scarlet-and-blue boats of Nazaré were
behind us as we drove back through Alcobaça and turned
northwest again along the highway to Fátima. We were in
mountain country now. Most of the vineyards were behind
us. Olive trees and giant windmills stood silhouetted against
the sky. The road was used by donkeys and oxcarts, and men
and women barefoot, with very few cars to be seen.

Since we intended to make a long visit to Fátima, and since we had the convenience of a car, we had been told that we would find our best accommodations at a *pensão*, or wayside inn, in the village of Aljubarrota. We were skeptical. Outside of the cities we had not seen many stopping places. When we heard that the rates for the best double room with bath and three meals a day would cost us $2.25 each, we shuddered inwardly.

But the Estalagem do Cruzeiro was a setting for a foreign romance. On a hill by the side of the road, with a view dropping away across miles of woodland to the crest of the cliff at Nazaré, it stood in colorful perfection. Wood-paneled rooms with wild flowers in every corner awaited us. A fire crackled in the lounge. Everyone from the innkeeper's baby to the chambermaid smiled a welcome.

And the food was good. That may sound like an unimportant, particularly unspiritual remark, but even pilgrims must eat. In Lisbon the cuisine is perfect. All over Portugal the meats are excellent. But we had already sampled out-of-town cooking, to our dismay. Portuguese palates are tuned to such dishes as soup served with a half inch of cold olive oil on top of it, and codfish in any guise at all, so long as it is steeped in olive oil. They favor poached eggs (poached with olive oil in the water) on top of soup, on top of codfish, and on top of steak. To avoid illness, it is vital for an American to find a cook who understands a foreigner's peculiar aversion to oil. We found one at the Estalagem.

A brawny-looking woman in an apron, holding a large wooden paddle, stood carved in bas-relief on the front wall of the inn. Proudly our driver explained that we were on the historic site of the battle of 1385, when Portugal finally defeated Spain.

"And who is the lady?"

"She was the baker's wife. For days she tended her husband's business while the battle surged back and forth across these hills. Finally she wearied of this waste of time. She took the long shovel used to place the loaves in the oven, and went out to fight. In no time she had killed all the Spaniards, and Portugal won."

"She did, eh?"

"Our Portuguese women are strong, Senhor Armstrong! And they stand for no nonsense."

We were less than thirty miles from Fátima, but night had closed over the mountains. The road ahead was winding and steep, and the good souls at the shrine would soon be asleep. We must wait till morning.

In the hall we overheard our driver speaking to the innkeeper, explaining why we had come to Portugal.

"They want to see the shrine of Our Lady of Fátima."

"Ah, yes. But why did they come so soon? This is only the seventh. Will they not stay for the thirteenth?"

"They say they will stay two weeks, maybe more."

"And they are Americans? I do not believe it. There is nothing at Fátima to keep an American here that long. That is why they go away without ever understanding really about Our Lady of Fátima."

Quietly we went down to dinner, and wondered.

Would we stay?

Chapter Six

THE ROAD TO FÁTIMA

Rain woke us early in the morning, the rain that was to become so integral a part of our pilgrimage that the sound of it drops constantly in our memories.

The rain we knew was unusual; the floods in Lisbon were front-page news. Ordinarily the spring and summer months in these mountains are dazzling and warm; weeks pass without a cloud. October is the start of the damp winter season; one can expect showers with fair frequency but no great intensity, a bit like the month of April in the United States.

For our pilgrimage, however, the rain fell as if sent to earth with a specific mission to perform. It conjured before our eyes the pictures we had seen of October 1917, when thousands waited in the storm to see a miracle. It whispered of the curious mixture of God's blessings with His chastisement, as the water that nourished the fields drenched the farmers who labored in them. It evoked a sadness, a yearning for the peace no storms can cloud.

Outside the inn the children of Aljubarrota were hurrying to school, laughing and singing as their bare feet squished through the puddles. Two men were turning the ropes and wheels of a stone well. The wood creaked and groaned with each turn of the wheel, five minutes of hard work to retrieve one bucket of water. The men were singing. Clouds hid the mountains, and mist blew in wraiths around the tall stone cross by the roadside from which the Estalagem do Cruzeiro draws its name.

Our road from Lisbon had been straight and gentle. From Aljubarrota onward we were in barren country, the rock-strewn range of the Serra da Aire, the mountains of the wind. The highway led through the red clay fields of the roof-tile makers, through tenacious farms of maize, and small patches of cabbage and kale. Then suddenly, as we swung around a wide bend in the road, through the mist and rain loomed the white towers of Batalha—the cathedral of victory, one of the most improbable and beautiful houses of God.

Standing in a hollow below the level of the village, the cathedral seems to float on an unseen lake, a mirage of beauty. It is built in what is called Manueline style, intricately carved, fantastically delicate and ornate. Every square foot is twisted into flowers and curlicues and figures, till you would swear the material was not limestone but a confection from the land of magic.

So large is the Cathedral of Our Lady of Victory that it dwarfs the town itself. We passed through the massive wooden doors and stood in silence. We had expected gloom and dampness. We stood instead in the center of light, pure and soft as the dawn. Immense white pillars held the high-flung starry vault over our heads. Slim, tall windows of stained glass transformed the gray of the storm into warm red and blue and shimmering yellow. Here John I, founder of Portugal, had given thanks to the Blessed Virgin nearly six hundred years ago. We added our prayer.

Past the tombs of John and his wife Philippa, daughter of the English John of Gaunt, and their son, Prince Henry the Navigator, we wandered through the spun-sugar arches of the Royal Cloister, where the Unknown Soldier lies. Before us lay the strangest sight of all—the Capelas Imperfeitas, the unfinished chapels. They were begun in the fifteenth century, these tall octagons of prayer, and never finished. They have no roofs. They stand in rich cream carving, open to the rain and sun, silent and unmolested.

Many stories are told of why they were not finished. The reason may be, as someone shyly suggested, that the Cathedral of Our Lady of Victory was only a beginning, the end of which was Fátima.

From the quiet of the chapels we drove through the market place of Batalha, bustling with chickens and pigs and garlic chains and olive oil, and the orange-and-purple baskets of the women.

We swerved a hairpin curve. Ahead stood a modest road sign:

FÁTIMA. 24 KILOMETERS.

The road is good, but dangerous to the uninitiated. Only two lanes wide, the pavement bends back on itself like a circus contortionist, skirting precipices with abandon. Traffic is heavy. Oxcarts and donkeys and flocks of sheep intermingle with brisk barefoot pedestrians.

Through the rain we stared at those mountains and wondered how men lived in such country. The ground looked like a boneyard, littered with gray-white stones. It seemed as if when God was through making the world He tossed the scrapings and leftovers of rocks here and abandoned them. New England's stoniest acres are smooth plowland compared to the fields around Fátima.

Ahead on a promontory, black against the sullen skies, stood a stark stone cross.

"We are entering the diocese of Leiria, which embraces Fátima," said our driver. "Soon we see the Way of the Cross. Fourteen crosses from here to the Basilica, and the people of my land walk it, some of them on their knees."

From the comfort of the back seat we asked: "How far is it, this Way of the Cross?"

"The first one is in the village of Reguengo do Fetal, a little less than nine of your miles from there to the sanctuary at Fátima."

"Nine miles on your knees?"

"You do not have to go on your knees. Not everyone does. Our Lady of Fátima asked for penance. There are many ways of doing penance. In my land people who want to, think it is a good sacrifice to make to God, to walk on their knees. You will see many of them at Fátima. I have heard your country-men say it is a horrible thing to do. Maybe. We do not think so. But maybe we think some things you do are foolish too. I don't know. In this world, in this Church, there is room for many kinds of people."

The first of the fourteen crosses rose out of the mist beyond the car window.

"The Bishop of Leiria permitted these to be built for the pilgrims in 1927," said the driver. "Each parish along the way paid for its own cross."

Cross by cross we rode toward Fátima, following in our mind's eye the path of agony of the Lord's arrest and trial and execution and death.

The road broadened into a wide rotary. New avenues led off in four directions, a meeting place for pilgrims from all parts of Portugal.

Against the gray clouds we saw the white spire of the Basilica, looking in the distance like a giant sister of some little white country church, humble and unassuming as it pointed skyward.

"Fátima!"

71

Chapter Seven

"FÁTIMA IS NOTHING!"

To come upon Fátima alone, in the rain, when pilgrims are absent, is like stumbling on a giant stage deserted after a performance—lonesome and bewildering.

We left the car and stood at the side of the vast square that fronts on the Basilica. The square is unadorned, paved in macadam. It has held one million pilgrims at a time, but when we came it was empty.

In the very center of the square is a stone column supporting a shining statue of the Sacred Heart of Jesus. On the left and right stand two hospitals; giant white colonnades are under construction to link them with the Basilica. It is as if the tall white church were the head of the Fátima devotion, the center from which activity springs. The hospitals with their colonnades stretch out like welcoming arms and helping hands.

But the heart of Fátima, like the heart of a man, is off center, slightly to the left in an otherwise perfect design.

The heart of Fátima lies in a crude small shed of stucco and wood. It is called the Chapel of the Apparitions, and it is built directly over the place where Our Lady appeared to the children.

The tree, the little holm oak, is gone. The first pilgrims in 1917 stripped it bare of leaves and branches, chopped off pieces of the trunk, leaving only a forlorn stump. Eventually that and even the roots were carried away. Today a cement column inside the chapel marks the spot where once the tiny oak had stood.

The chapel is utterly plain. There is a cubicle about six feet square containing an altar where visiting priests from all over the world say Mass every half hour in the mornings. Exactly three people at a time can kneel at the Communion rail. Above the altar stands the original and most-loved statue of Our Lady of Fátima.

In 1920 that statue was placed in the first chapel ever built on this spot, smuggled there in a cart full of farm tools for fear of government officials. In 1922 that first chapel was dynamited by the more rabid atheists of the regime. Five bombs were used to destroy the chapel. Four exploded. The one at the roots of the holm oak, at the foot of the statue, never went off.

The statue now is kept in a niche over the altar, backed with fan pleats of faded green satin, edged around with slightly dilapidated artificial flowers. The altar cloth and fittings are of a simplicity seldom seen outside a mission church.

Aside from the closed-in altar cubicle, the chapel is nothing more than a shed open on all four sides and roofed with tile.

It provides a few folding chairs and kneeling room for perhaps twenty people. On the walls of the cubicle are set the typical discreet plaques of thanksgiving carved in all languages: "Obrigada, Nossa Senhora da Fátima." "Merci, Notre Dame." "Thank you to Our Lady." "In gratitude to Our Lady, from five of us who were in Buchenwald."

We knelt awhile to pray in the chapel, but as we rose again we had to confess our disappointment. There is nothing to look at really in the chapel. We began to understand why Americans do not linger in the bleak, ardently undramatized shrine. Yet we were ashamed. We had the feeling the fault was ours.

Hopefully we turned our faces to the Basilica. The mountain wind whipped the rain into our faces.

The word "basilica" in Greek means royal. In our time it is a title given by the Pope to certain privileged churches outstanding either for their antiquity or for other spiritual reasons. As we walked toward it we remembered that this slope where now it stood was the place where Lucy and Jacinta and Francisco had been playing at building a house before the first apparition. They had built quite a house!

We climbed the long cascade of white marble stairs and paused before a sign warning all women that in Portugal proper dress for church includes long sleeves as well as a head covering, a rule severely enforced. We pushed open the wooden door and found ourselves in a church unlike any other in design. At Fátima there are fourteen side altars as well as the main one—fifteen, one for each mystery of the rosary.

In the half-light that filtered through the tall windows, gleaming bronze carvings over each altar recalled the great scenes of the life of Mary in which men for centuries have found deep lessons of the Way and the Truth.

Here was Mary the maiden, humble in the moment of the Annunciation by the angel Gabriel. "Hail Mary, full of grace, blessed art thou among women." Here was Mary the Mother, in the stable at Bethlehem. Mary at the foot of the Cross. Mary in the wonder of her Son's Resurrection. Mary assumed into heaven, crowned queen of all saints. A life, and a death, in the love and presence of Jesus.

We walked slowly forward. At each of the front side altars, inside the rail, stood a small tomb, unimposing in design. Even in the gloom we could read the names carved on the chaste stone. Jacinta and Francisco lay here.

We knelt by the altar. Around us huddled the silent, omnipresent forms of old women in black shawls and veils, praying, giving to God the hours which were the sole treasure left them to offer.

But we were restless and damp. The chill of uncarpeted stone filled our lungs and settled into our legs. Our knees hurt. Shame-faced over our lack of devotion, we left the Basilica.

Was it for this that we had traveled so far? What did we expect to find at Fátima, after all?

Unspoken questions pursued us like the rain as we hastened across the rough pasture land behind the hospital in search of the one other place in Fátima of which we had heard, the Seminário das Missões. Before we left, we had the good fortune to meet Father John De Marchi, author of the finest histories of Fátima. A smiling, informal little man from Italy, Father De Marchi had lived in Portugal for years. He had, at the age of thirty-one, founded this seminary for his order. The Consolata Fathers, an order of missionaries rooted in Turin, have become an integral part of the community of Fátima. Father De Marchi had assured us that they would welcome us at the seminary, and even during the avalanche of pilgrims on the thirteenth would take care of all our needs.

Shivering and dripping and disconsolate of soul, we made our way to the door. In that black hour we were ready to admit spiritual defeat, confess our disappointment, and go home. What had we really to hope for from stranger priests?

We had forgotten that, no matter who or where you are, no priest is a stranger.

We rang the bell. A boy in a black suit answered. He took our rather damp letter of introduction and waved us into a waiting room.

We shook our clothes, and dried our faces, and stood dripping casually onto the floor. We paced up and down. Then idly we glanced at the overstuffed autograph albums on the table. Every language we had ever seen, and many we had not, were there. In dialects of India and China, of Arabia and Tanganyika, in Italian, Spanish, English, and French, pilgrims had written of their fervent devotion to Our Lady of Fátima. The names of policemen and GIs, financiers and stenographers, bank clerks and philosophers followed one another. Ex-King Umberto of Italy. Don Juan, pretender to the Spanish throne. The Pope's sister. Bishop Fulton Sheen. A Russian airman who escaped to find true freedom in Our Lord's service . . .

The noiseless arrival of a tall young priest interrupted us, the presence of a man who in his early thirties is rector of this

77

seminary and who carries with him an indefinable air of grace and serenity.

With a smile he welcomed us: "I am Father Aldo Mongiano. What can I do for you?"

It was a rhetorical question. We did not need to tell him what we wanted. He sent our coats to dry in the kitchen, produced large cups of well-meant, if undrinkable, coffee, and asked us what we had seen and what we planned to do.

"You like Fátima?" he asked at last with a twinkle in his brown eyes. "Maybe no. Maybe not yet. There is not much to see here, and it is not very beautiful. But stay awhile, and perhaps we can help you to see why we like it here."

He paused, and his long thin hands stroked his bony chin. "Some people come here and say: 'Why would the Mother of God come to a place like this? It is not beautiful like Lourdes, nor historical like Palestine. Fátima is nothing.'"

His laugh warmed the bare refectory like springtime. "Perhaps," he said, "that is the answer. She came here because Fátima is nothing. Because the people and the place are so simple that she could be believed. It is a mystery, perhaps?"

Chapter Eight

THE PEOPLE OF FÁTIMA

Rain seemed to possess the mountains as the perfume of new-mown grass can possess the air of a summer noontide. The rain was inescapable and almost silent. It was accepted by the inhabitants of Fátima without comment. They moved in it with complete serenity, barefoot and calm.

We were neither barefoot nor calm.

With a trilingual priest from the seminary, Father Francis Maggioni, we were on our way to Aljustrel for our first glimpse of the homes and relatives of the three children.

We were definitely odd-looking, even by American standards. We carried enough equipment slung or lashed to us to weight down a burro. Almost every step of the way each day we carried between us two still cameras, one movie camera, one light meter, a canvas bag of film and filters, one pair of binoculars, a stack of six or seven chocolate bars perpetually renewed, a jar of instant coffee, sunglasses, three notebooks, five pens and many pencils, and one trunk-like pocketbook holding everything from plastic rainboots, make-up, and cigarettes to rosaries and a pocket dictionary. We were far from representing the modern streamlined traveler of the fashion magazines.

But to Portuguese eyes we were not merely ungainly beasts of burden (how gracefully they carry their own paraphernalia, neatly packed in baskets atop their heads). We were fantastic giants, weird, if likable, members of another race. The Portuguese indulge in a national pastime which can be described in English only as "staring." For practice they stare at each other, but we were specimens truly worthy of their talent. They stared at us with fascination and unconcealed delight. Strangely, we found it hard to resent.

In the first place, we are tall, both of us in the neighborhood of six feet, give or take an inch. The Portuguese countryfolk average little more than five feet tall. And although our taste is not garish, we admittedly do wear colors—a blue coat, perhaps, or a wine-and-gray tie. They wear black, with sometimes a dash of dark brown.

One perilously rainy afternoon we sludged down the mud road to Aljustrel, attired in what seemed to us fairly appropriate clothes. We came quietly but not unobserved. From the houses and the chicken coops a group of women appeared at once, whispering and staring. In no time they had surrounded April in solemn conclave. Their heads came a good three inches below her shoulders. She stood with the rain beating down, smiling with what she hoped was a judicious combination of courtesy and aplomb. Barefooted, they moved among the swelling puddles, clucking their tongues and darting anxious glances at her. Finally one gentle old lady seized the tip of her raincoat sleeve and peered up underneath.

"Ah!" she cried.

She held it out for all to witness that April was also wearing a white sweater underneath the coat. Gradually we understood. Her raincoat is red plaid with pretty silver buttons. But they had never heard of using plaid for a coat, and it worried them to see a girl in such a downpour wearing what must obviously be a party dress!

Their relief at the discovery of the sweater was only temporary. They were busy again with another problem. Chattering anxiously, they bent down to examine April's feet. Feeling a little foolish, April did her best to explain in pidgin Portuguese that she was simply wearing plastic boots to protect her shoes from the rain. The only response she got was a pitying look and a curiously tender pat on the arm—and the continual hum of concern.

Not for two whole days did April solve the mystery of her feet. Again it was raining, and she walked quietly into the Chapel of the Apparitions to hear Mass. Thunder may roll and babies cry and turkeys run loose through the square, and not one Portuguese woman will look up from her prayers. But April's entrance in plastic overshoes caused a buzz of excitement.

A bilingual priest beside her turned and smiled.

"For the sake of peace and quiet, you had best remove your

boots. The white plastic is a new sight to them, and they have concluded that those gadgets are bandages and that you are here for a cure. How brave you are, they are saying, to walk on such evidently painful feet!"

No matter how they stared, the people of Fátima and of all Portugal, without exception, were kind and gracious hosts. There is a saying in Europe, "He is as polite as a Portuguese." They are unexcelled in the art of human kindness to each other and to all strangers.

One particular day we took refuge from a sudden torrent from the sky under a tree near a small white home. Instantly the man of the house beckoned us in. In the cramped front room his entire family was gathered, his mother, his wife, and seven children, most of them, like ourselves, oozing puddles with every move. There was only one chair, and the rain blowing through the door had soaked it. The wife ran to the next room to bring a fine dry chair. Dripping coats and all, she insisted we sit on it.

We had only one small chocolate bar left. After some deliberation Martin gave it to one of the middle-sized girls. In wide-eyed ceremony she opened the paper, broke off a large piece, whirled around, and popped it into her wizened grandmother's toothless mouth. Each child, each parent was given a bite, and without a whimper the girl ate what was left as her share, a morsel no longer than half an inch. We learned later that it was the first chocolate she or her brothers and sisters had ever tasted.

Never in Fátima could you feel lonely. This is no ordinary shrine, a place set apart. In Fátima there are no guides, no tours, no peddlers, no beggars. The Bishop of Leiria has struggled manfully against all pressure groups to keep Fátima free from any mercenary, worldly taint. There is a sanctuary, chapel, and Basilica and its staff; about a dozen seminaries, convents, and monasteries; some *pensãos* and three or four shops; and the newly built homes of a few devout souls who wish only to live in the peace of the Cova. But even without an interpreter you feel at one with the people who have always lived here, the people of Aljustrel. No one will pass you without a greeting: *"Boas dias!"*

It is a lesson in simplicity and brotherhood just to be there and to answer, *"Boas dias!"* Here every man is your neighbor.

One afternoon we were to stand alone in a corridor of the hospital with Senhor José Thedim, sculptor of the Fátima statue. Our interpreter had momentarily deserted us. We smiled at Senhor Thedim. And he smiled at us. The moment stretched taut and uncomfortable as our smiles. We could hardly air the Portuguese small talk we had learned; a sculptor would care little for our views on dinner menus, and we had already told him who we were and why we had come. He spoke no English. What could we say?

Suddenly Senhor Thedim's polite smile vanished before a look of wise understanding. He shrugged away the barriers of speech.

"A lingua do rosário é universal!" he said.

In that moment we understood another part of the truth of Fátima, the modern answer to the tragedy of Babel. At the United Nations Building in New York, men have contrived intricate systems of translating one speaker's words into all the myriad tongues of his listeners. The delegates sit with headphones, physically together, but each still separate in his own world.

At Fátima no machines are needed, only a small string of beads and a crucifix. The rosary is a language in itself, and no man is alone, for all are children of God.

In such understanding there can be peace.

Chapter Nine

"COME INTO OUR HOUSE!"

To reach the children's home, you go down the main road toward the parish church of Fátima and turn off onto a simple country lane of clay and rocks and weeds. One kilometer along that path you find a huddle of ten or twelve homes. That is the entire village of Aljustrel.

The houses, like those all over Portugal's countryside, are of white stucco. The roofs are brownish-red tile; many of them have a pagoda-like slant to the eaves and tiny oriental peaks and grillworks, mute vestiges of Moorish influence. Every house has its own vegetable garden, chicken coop, and rabbit hutch. Donkeys live in the back yards. Here and there are pigs and sheep or a cow.

In the center of Aljustrel stand two houses a little plainer than the rest. On one side of the road is the present home of the Martos, parents of Jacinta and Francisco. Across from it is the house where they used to live, where the children were born. Today one of their surviving sons and his wife make their home there.

Father Maggioni, our Consolata friend and interpreter, is a habitué of the Marto household. He called out:

"Ti Marto!"

A small, grinning, grizzled man came to the wooden gate. He wears a long black stocking cap, the *carapuça*, which serves all the mountain men as head covering and carry-all for tobacco and lunch. He wears an incredibly patched suit. Once a brown pin stripe, it is mended all over in blue and black and gray serge. A costume designer would reject the outfit as exaggerated, but nothing could more perfectly convey the unself-conscious poverty and the comfortable dignity of his life. His only ornaments are a lapel button of a Catholic farmers' guild and a large pocket watch attached to his vest by a broad black ribbon.

His full name is Manuel Pedro Marto, but the world has come to call him by the affectionate title first given him by our friend, Father De Marchi. He is Ti Marto—Uncle Marto.

Ti Marto is the father of the two younger children of the vision, the two whose tombs stand silent in the Basilica. The Church has already made the first moves toward the public official declaration that his Francisco and Jacinta are saints. Because of the children he sired and raised and buried, the parish of Fátima has become famous. Yet by his own choice he lives in this cottage, still working with his hands to support his wife. He is eighty-two years old.

From behind him steps an even tinier figure, an old lady wearing a faded brown dress, a clean black apron, and a black kerchief over her hair. Her face is gnarled and gullied with time, but her toothless smile is bright as a vigil light. This is Tia Olympia, the eighty-four-year-old mother who long ago taught Francisco and Jacinta their first "Hail Mary."

Father Maggioni asked with a smile: "May we see your palace?"

"Ah, my palace! It is so grand, so magnificent! Come in!" Ti Marto chuckled.

We passed through the yard strewn with layers of fresh pine needles and brush. We wiped our feet on the threshold. The wall by the door is hung with an array of holy pictures, including the Martos' two children and Lucy.

Tia Olympia darted over to us and without ceremony bent down, skillfully plucking a thread draggling from the hem of April's dress. We started to protest, but the look on her face stopped us. We had been adopted, and who dares complain when a mother fusses over you?

With a smile she led us into the parlor. It is a small window-less room furnished with a massive hand-hewn chest and two stools, and a handsome clock that does not run. From the chest Tia Olympia produced a loaf of dark bread to show us her handwork. Like all Portuguese bread, it was heavier than wood, rich with unrefined goodness.

Beyond the parlor is a smaller room with a few candles burning on a small table. There is no electricity. Tacked to the wall are the treasures of the family, a letter of blessing from the Pope, lithographs of Our Lady, a few photographs of the children, some newspaper clippings, and their rosaries dangling from a nail.

The bedrooms are closet size and windowless. The kitchen, with the generous kettle and staunch earthenware jugs, is lit by a skylight less than a foot square. No one could imagine a poorer dwelling. Surely the parish could provide better quarters for this old couple? In English, which neither Ti Marto nor Tia Olympia can understand, we asked Father Maggioni.

"People who come here always try to give them money. They always refuse. They say they have everything they want. When money is forced on them they take it to the shrine, or else stand on the main road looking for some really poor person to give it to."

We nodded. We had the feeling that solemnity was expected of us, big gawking luxury-lovers that we were, stooped under the low ceiling of this bare dark home.

We turned toward the door and laughed out loud.

When we first came in we had shed our cameras and other burdens, such as April's gargantuan pocketbook, in the parlor. Ti Marto had been curious. Now he stood posed elegantly in the courtyard, the black patent-leather bag slung over his arm. With a waggle of his hips he pirouetted through the cabbage patch and back to hand it to April with a bow and a wide yellow-toothed grin.

He spoke to Father Maggioni in Portuguese.

"He says: 'Baskets on the head are better, but this is more fun. And laughter is good.'"

Who could feel solemn in the Marto home?

Down the lane a way stands another house, the home of Lucy. Her parents are dead, and she herself is in the Carmel in Coimbra, but her sister, Maria dos Anjos, still lives here with her children and grandchildren.

Lucy's house is as plain as the Martos', box-shaped, with two small windows flanking the wooden door. With her apron Maria dos Anjos swept a path through the children on the front steps. We entered the parlor. Directly off it is the room where Lucy was born and where her mother died. The simple metal-framed bed, the wooden cradle, the crucifix, the gaily embroidered pillow are still in use. Babies are still born here, Lucy's nieces and nephews, and their children as well. Off to the side is a handloom for rugs and blankets. One of the nieces looked up from her work and smiled.

Lucy grew up here, youngest of seven children in what most people would call a grossly underprivileged home. Maria dos Anjos, our tired, practical-faced hostess, was her oldest sister.

"She loved to be cuddled, Lucy did. She would run to Mother and sit on her lap to be cuddled and kissed, even when she was ten years old. We used to tease her and even be cross with her, but it made no difference. When my first baby was born Lucy ran as fast as she could to get there and clutched the baby and covered it with kisses. Not like the others around here, who thought a baby was just a baby."

Maria dos Anjos, Mary of the Angels, at first did not put much stock in her little sister's tale of seeing both the angels and Mary out in the pasture so long ago. It is always hard to believe wonders about those near you. Today she believes. But you feel that for her the apparitions of Fátima are the supreme mystery of faith. *To her little sister?* A picture of Lucy in the dress of a Dorothean nun is framed near the doorway. Maria dos Anjos stood by it as she talked to us,

89

unquestioning, accepting. But amazement still lurked in her eyes after all these years.

We stepped over and around the covey of her grandchildren. Father Maggioni was beckoning us back up the road to see the house where Jacinta and Francisco were born.

The room where the boy died of influenza is also still in use, clean and neat, virtually unchanged. The children had no belongings to leave behind for curious, relic-seeking eyes. What clothes and playthings they had were exhausted by use. In their mother's room, where they were born, only one new thing has been added, an inexpensive statue of Our Lady of Fátima. The same cross, leaning with age, still stands in the deepset, shuttered window over a plain, wooden chest. Beside the skinny brass bed a wooden chair with a faded plaid pillow sits patiently.

None of these houses is a museum or a shrine. The children who scuffled and laughed and dreamed inside these walls and who saw the Queen of Heaven are gone. Other children toss pillows in sham battle, weep and giggle, and collect fireflies and spiders here, and kneel on the bare floor by these bedsteads to pray.

"You would like to talk to Ti Marto further, I am sure," said Father Maggioni. "But the thirteenth is so soon, and many people will be coming to see him. So I have made an appointment with him for Sunday afternoon for you. Not that Ti Marto is as self-important as that. But you will see how many come."

"Does everybody get to talk to him?"

"Everybody. He never says no. People have been walking uninvited through Tia Olympia's house for thirty-six years, ever since 1917, poking their noses where they will. They grin at the Martos like they were freaks, and touch them as if they were magic, and make general nuisances of themselves. It's always worst around the thirteenth."

"That's martyrdom, to have no privacy," said Martin.

Father Maggioni nodded. Raindrops skipped off his black beret and down his tortoise-shell glasses.

"They belong to the world because God happened to choose two of their children. They've never yet complained."

We are people who savor the luxury of being able to close our doors and be alone when we want. We began to feel abashed at our own desire to see into these people's lives and ask questions.

The priest answered our unspoken thought.

"They do not mind. They take it as their job in life. For what else is important in their lives?"

Chapter Ten

THE ROCK OF THE ANGEL

Back at the Consolata Seminary, the rector, Father Aldo, presented us with another invaluable friend, a Scotsman come to study in Fátima for the priesthood. Hugh Ferguson is a compact figure of a man with a large soul, a disarming laugh, and an unforgettable accent.

"I'll be wi' ye in a mooment," he said. "I promised to help a Dominican find his byge."

"What's a Dominican doing with a bike?"

"Noo, noo, you do na' understand." He smiled. "He has lost his byge. B-a-g, byge!"

As the rain paused for its afternoon siesta, we took off again through the mud with Hugh in the lead. He was taking us to where as yet no churches stand, to the spots the people in these parts treasure as natural shrines.

Back down the lane and through Aljustrel we trudged. As we passed Lucy's house, her nieces and nephews ran out to greet us, trailing along like a company of sparrows through the cold mist. We went up past the vegetable garden behind her house till we came to a good-sized, stone-lined well. Set low in the ground, it is actually only a cistern to store rain water, and since it was full at the time, boards and stones covered the top. A few olive trees, almonds, and figs stood round it for shade.

The children clambered unconcernedly over the well. One little boy, Antonio, or Tonico, as his pet name was, stood on the boards and stared back at us. He was rounder and heavier than the pictures of Francisco, and a little younger. But his feet were just as happily stained with mud, and his dark eyes twinkled.

"If you remember, it was at this well that the angel surprised the children at play. It was his second appearance to them," said Hugh.

We looked at Tonico. A child's eyes might readily see into another world. Did not Jesus say that to enter His kingdom we must become as little children?

The sound of their play followed us as Hugh led the way on down a lane, out of sight of the houses. The ground grew rougher, more rock than earth, skeleton-gray in the fog. The hills here are laced with low stone walls isolating each tiny field. The complication of inheritance laws in Portugal has carved the plots even smaller. One family's holdings will be scattered in walled-in fragments over many miles of hills, and each fragment has its own name.

We scrambled over the stones into a field scarcely different from its neighbors. It is about a hundred yards square, a low-walled pasture called Valinhos.

On the wall near the lane is one of the tiniest shrines in the world, homemade and almost camouflaged by the stones.

"This is where Our Lady appeared to the children on August nineteenth, right after they were released from Mayor Santos' jail, you know."

A small cement-covered box, upended and open on one side, serves as a niche. Inside are two of the common inexpensive statues of Our Lady, one about a foot tall, the other much smaller, seemingly added as an afterthought. Four little glass vases with rain-beaten fresh flowers encircled them.

"The larger statue is cemented in because the—uh—good strangers who come here have a tendency to collect souvenirs. And the people of Aljustrel can't afford a new statue every week."

"Who built this?"

"No one knows definitely. They all take turns tending it. They like it this way, simple, just as it used to be practically. They feel it's theirs especially. You remember that when Our Lady came here Lucy had to send John to fetch Jacinta. For many it was the turning point of belief. The pasture at the Cova is all changed, but Valinhos is the same. Nice, isn't it?"

A small girl passed solemnly and silently down the lane. She was no older than Jacinta had been that August in 1917. Barefoot, in white blouse, brown skirt, and diminutive shawl, she seemed for a moment to be a child out of the past, blessed with vision and glory.

"People come here often to say the rosary," said Hugh. "It's more private. And for some it's easier to understand the message here in the fields than in the chapel or the Basilica, as grand as that is."

A swift spurt of rain drove us to shelter under a spreading holm-oak tree.

Valinhos is a desolate spot. God has not lavished greenery or flowers on it. It seems to have stood from the beginning of time, barren and bleak, softened only by the gentle encroachment of grass upon the moldering rock. But the air is sweet there, and the wind is fresh as the day of creation. There is a blessing on it that weaves its way through the tension of the modern soul, unlocking it to the whispers of God. In Valinhos you believe that if you could become as a child again, if you could be reborn, you could hear the voice of heaven.

The shower passed. Hugh took us on up the road. The olive trees were shaggy with age. In the mist they loomed like gray-robed monks poised in hermits' silence. The rutted lane gave way to a grass path bending up a slope past a weather-beaten sign pointing to Aljustrel, to Valinhos, and upward to the Cabeço. The rocks, moss-gray, lay in passive confusion, as if dropped by a giant, impatient hand.

Ahead stood a little promontory, the Cabeço, a child-size natural fortress of rock. One venerable olive with still living branches flings its hollow trunk in a wide arc of shelter. Everything is gray—sky, and rock, and tree—wind-beaten, secret-ridden as the rocks and trees of Gethsemane. But in the center of the Cabeço is one strangely white stone, about two and a half feet tall, almost theatrical in its natural prominence.

"This land belonged to Lucy's godfather. The field down there belonged to her parents. The children liked to eat lunch here while the sheep grazed below. This was where the angel appeared the first time and also the third, and last, time."

We climbed to the white rock. Beside it is a small space of plain dirt, just large enough for three small children.

"Over this rock on the third visit the angel placed the Blessed Sacrament and the Chalice. He knelt here with them before giving them Holy Communion."

The white stone stands like a primordial altar. It is absolutely unchanged. Not even a marker has been added.

Standing there, you remember your own childhood. You remember the hours when a pile of ancient rock could become a shelter for the fragile dreams of your soul. You remember, too, how close heaven seemed in the long days of youth. There were no barriers then to shutter the truth from your heart. God was part of your breathing, pulsing through you whether you forgot Him in your play or threw yourself at Him in a silent ecstasy of prayer.

People forget as they grow older how beautiful was prayer as a child. They come to believe that a child does not know how to pray because he is always asking God for the little things he wants immediately, urgently. Loftily they construct an ethics, a science of prayer, involute and scheduled. So many of us are proud of the adultness of our relationship to the God who is known as Father. We forget that He must place special value on the little ones; He even chose to be one Himself.

In the distance a rooster crowed. The fog had lifted, leaving a ceiling of pearl-gray. From the Cabeço we could see all of Aljustrel, spread out like a miniature village, incidental to the fields and rocks that God had made. We could hear the bleat of sheep and a donkey singing. Raising our eyes, we could see on the horizon the simple white tower of the parish church at Fátima.

The hour was late, but we did not want to leave. We had the feeling that if we waited we might find the invisible door of the soul that opens back on the innocence of childhood. And we found ourselves praying that our Father would lead us back to the love and intensity and trust we had left behind in the years.

We could feel peace settling on our souls as we left the Cabeço.

Chapter Eleven

GUARDIAN OF THE SECRET

That night we were to meet the Bishop of Leiria, whose diocese includes Fátima and Aljustrel.

Leiria had no bishop in the days of the apparitions. The Church in Portugal had been outlawed in 1910. But in May 1920, Pope Benedict XV restored the old diocese of Leiria and appointed a new bishop, His Excellency, Dom José Alves Correia da Silva.

He had chosen no ordinary priest to whom to entrust the destiny of Fátima. Dom José, then forty-three, possessed extraordinary education and deep devotion to Our Lady. His people love to tell of him that in the persecution he was forced to stand for grim, endless hours in water so cold that his legs came close to freezing. Today he is a cripple, confined to a wheel chair. Through prayer to Our Lady of Sorrows, he won his freedom from the Republic, and in gratitude he made six pilgrimages to Lourdes to implore Our Lady's help for Portugal before ever lightning flashed in the Cova.

As Bishop of Leiria in 1920, Dom José took over the problems of Fátima. He it was who sent Lucy away to the boarding school and eventually to the Dorothean convent. He was the one who set up the commission to investigate the truth of the apparitions. A devout man, but cautious, he did not issue his formal approval of the cult until October 1930, exactly thirteen years after the Miracle of the Sun.

Slowly under his conservative leadership Fátima has grown. From the first he has been determined that no taint of commercialism shall mar this shrine. Staunchly and humbly he has resisted every attempt to introduce what his critics say are only "modern conveniences." There are no hotels in Fátima, no restaurants, only a few bare *pensãos* and hospices, and five or six quietly run religious shops. The only new buildings he has permitted are monasteries and convents and a few private homes. No one will make a fortune out of Our Lady of Fátima as long as Dom José lives.

To this man Lucy has entrusted the one remaining secret which Our Lady gave to her.

We drove through the dark winding road from Fátima to the town of Leiria. It was a bit crowded physically and linguistically in the car. Besides ourselves and the driver, we had with us Father Aldo, the Italian rector of Consolata; Hugh Ferguson, our Scotch friend; and another pilgrim like ourselves, Father Ado Trabold, a German-born priest traveling on a British passport, returning to Europe for the first time in twenty-four years after working in Korea and Tanganyika.

Even at night the shadowy towers of the Moorish castle that tops the skyline of Leiria are breath-taking. This is a town redolent of age, once the residence of Queen St. Elizabeth of Portugal, a woman wise in the ways of making and keeping peace among nations.

Yet the residence of the Bishop of Leiria is far from grand. When Dom José arrived to restore the diocese he found the traditional episcopal palace had been used as a barracks and government offices. He had other things to do besides build a new home. Like the Martos, his manner of life has remained untouched by the popularity of Fátima. He makes no attempt to cater to the world that peers curiously into his affairs.

Two commonplace shops of tenants flank the entrance to his house. We passed through the street door directly into a stair well adorned with walls which were once painted to resemble marble and are now fading. At the head of the wooden stairs a little barefoot maid opened another door and showed us into the reception room.

In the center of one wall stood an old and elegant episcopal throne, obviously little used. Overhead, a ceiling of gilt filigree and tile, survivor of revolutions and republics, recalled another era. The walls were hung with framed oriental silk embroideries of roosters and chickens and flowers. Dainty muslin-covered chairs were ranged on every side. On the antique sofa lay freshly plumped new pillows of a vivid and questionable pink and blue. We did not sit down.

The maid returned to escort us down the narrow, dark hall to the Bishop's study. We stood in the doorway hesitantly. Until our eyes adjusted, we literally could not find him in that room.

His office is an absent-minded professor's paradise. Musty, book-lined, it boasts four tall windows, firmly boarded shut. Tables and chairs are buried beneath papers and pamphlets and towers of books. Yet what seems to be chaos proves to be uniquely in order. Just as a carpenter litters his workshop with shavings and sawdust and odd pieces of wood to be used at a later date, so this indefatigable priest surrounds himself with the ingredients of his mountainous labors. It is a comfortable, reassuringly human room.

A wheel chair waited near the door. The Bishop himself was seated behind a small desk in the dimness of the far left corner, smiling at our bewilderment.

At seventy-six, Dom José is helplessly infirm. His fingers are swollen and cold, and his left eye is affected. His smile is beautiful. The round, clear-skinned face under his thin white hair speaks of peace and the happiness of hard work. The shadow that crosses it now and then is more of pity grown from wisdom than it is of pain. His one good eye is alert, and appraising, and indescribably kind.

He speaks no English, and our Portuguese was still poverty-stricken. Cautiously we embarked on a long chain of translation. We asked our questions in English. Little Hugh with his thick burr phrased them in Italian. Father Aldo nodded and relayed them to the Bishop in Portuguese. Occasionally Father Trabold, who speaks Swahili, Korean, Chinese, German, French, and English, would ask a question of his own. He spoke directly to the Bishop in Latin.

Still, we made progress. After the amenities of our multilingual greetings and explanations of our visit, we began to ask the Bishop what he thought of the message of Fátima. Could it really bring peace to the world? Here was a man who had seen Communism win an agonizing grip on his own country, had suffered torture under the persecution, and had seen peace and God return to his homeland.

"How responsible is Our Lady of Fátima for the change in Portugal? Or would Communism have died a natural death without her?"

"Never! She alone has saved our land," came the answer. "She is responsible for all that has happened, completely. For every change. Political. Moral. Social. Spiritual."

"If the rest of the world were to follow Fátima's message, as Portugal has, would there be peace?"

A smile of pity for such a question.

"Of course!"

"Each part of the secret that has been revealed has added to our knowledge of the world's destiny between peace and war. The last, unopened secret is, we understand, in your care?"

"Yes."

"We have heard that there is a copy of the letter in which Lucy wrote the secret, a copy in the Vatican?"

"No. There is no copy. And no one has read it. I have the secret, and I have not read it."

"What," we asked timidly, "if it got lost, or destroyed?"

"Why should it? How could it? And Lucy is still alive. She could write it again."

The Bishop looked up and smiled as a handsome, tall, arrestingly expressive priest entered. Here, said the Bishop's glance, is the man to answer your questions. This was Canon Galamba, the Bishop's right hand and alter ego. Himself a writer of great note, he speaks fluent English and understands the foreign turn of mind. Energy flows from him. He moves over the whole room as he talks, leaning on tables to emphasize a point, then moving lithely on as if to keep pace with his thoughts.

"The secret? The letter? Ah." He grinned. "So many stories about the secret. That the Holy Father read it and fainted. That a copy is buried in a time bomb. So many stories, all wrong. It is here, without a copy, and I see by your eyes that you wonder how we will ever find it in this—uh—confusion."

"Or in a fire?" asked Father Trabold. "If Lucy is dead and the letter is gone, what will you do? Has the secret so little importance that you do not make a copy?"

"You have heard," asked Canon Galamba, "that the secret cannot be opened till 1960?"

We nodded. On that one date every report had agreed.

"That is not quite true. The Bishop could open it at any time he wishes. Now. Yesterday. Even years ago. But he will not."

One foot poised on a chair, Canon Galamba leaned forward.

"I was with him visiting Lucy one day years ago. Lucy said that now she could reveal the last part of the secret if the Bishop wanted her to. He did not want to hear it. He asked her finally to write it down and seal it. He could have read it then, but he would not. So Lucy agreed. But she made him promise that it would definitely be opened and released to the world at her death, or in 1960, whichever came first."

"But why doesn't he want to know what it is? Why doesn't he tell the world what it is?"

"I asked him that many times," said Canon Galamba. "And

always he says: 'It is not for me to interfere. Heaven's secrets are not for me, and I do not want that responsibility too.' "

Father Trabold, the pilgrim missionary, was braver than we.

"Doesn't that mean he is shirking his responsibility?" he asked.

"No. He believes that if God wanted it revealed right now, He would have said so specifically. Lucy only said she could reveal it now if the Bishop asked. She did not say it must be now. The dates were set after a discussion between the Bishop and Lucy."

For a moment silence sat in that dim warm room beside us. A million questions buzzed in our minds. Finally April spoke.

"If it were me, I would have opened it right away!"

Canon Galamba's lips twitched as he translated her words to the Bishop. A smile wrinkled that patient, old face as Dom José leaned toward her and spoke in the gentlest of tones.

"He says," Canon Galamba laughed, " 'That is why they do not make women bishops, my child!' "

The Bishop spoke again. To both of us the love in his voice needed no interpretation.

"He says he hopes he will see you again, after the thirteenth, after you have seen more of the shrine."

Canon Galamba did not translate what we are sure was the Bishop's unspoken thought:

"Come back when you have learned to understand a little more of Our Lady of Fátima!"

We kissed his ring and asked his blessing and left. Outside in the town square, Father Aldo spoke.

"You know, he has a way with heaven. Ever since I came to the seminary here I have heard about it. He refused government aid in building the Basilica. This is a very poor diocese. But he said: 'I made a contract with Our Lady. She will give me the money, and I will spend it for her. She knows best how to do things.' "

As our car pulled away into the darkness, no light showed through the shuttered windows of that study. Yet somehow we could both still see that smile, the smile of a man whose body cannot walk but whose soul soars.

Chapter Twelve

THE MAN IN THE CHICKEN COOP

Sunday afternoon we went to talk to Ti Marto.

The rain persisted. Red mud clung to our ankles. Our water-repellent coats felt as if they were woven out of fresh seaweed. Yet strangely we were neither miserable nor cold.

Father Maggioni, our Consolata guide, looking like some haphazard Benedictine in his stiff plastic coat and hood, set a brisk pace down the road to Aljustrel.

We could see why Ti Marto had made a special appointment for this interview. Already pilgrims arriving for the thirteenth, only two days away, were converging on Aljustrel, and every newcomer seemed determined to talk to him personally.

The little old man, now dressed in his best black Sunday suit, stepped out of a doorway like a conspirator. Taking off his black stocking cap, he tugged at Father Maggioni's sleeve and beckoned us to follow.

We entered the Marto yard. People crowded the tiny doorway, chattering and peering into the house. They did not notice us as we pushed open another gate into the vegetable patch. Ti Marto spoke to Father Maggioni, pointing to the lean-to shed in the corner of the garden behind a wall.

"He says if the lady does not mind we can sit in the chicken house. No one will know we are there and no one will interrupt."

Ti Marto had shooed the chickens away and carried out three wooden chairs for us. He himself sat on the chopping block. At our shoulder level plump rabbits munched cabbage leaves in their cage. A pigeon walked delicately behind our necks. Rain tapped tirelessly on the leaves of the fig tree outside and ran in small waterfalls off the eaves. But no wind entered here. It was a cozy place to be.

We had only a short list of questions. Interrogators far more skillful than we had covered the ground over and over in the past; we had read fifteen published versions of this man's testimony. But there were a few queries that to us personally were important. With the help of Father Maggioni, that sympathetic master of Italian, English, and Portuguese, we began our interview.

"What do you think of all the changes made here since 1917? Some people say it is not modern enough. Others say it should have been left alone, just the way it was when Our Lady came."

He shrugged. "Many were against the changes. Many asked me, 'Ti Marto, why the changes?' Well, one thing leads to another. We must let it grow up. For us who live here, it has been a confusion. Like when a shoemaker makes a pair of shoes. First it is all pieces and scraps, and then he puts it all together and it is shoes. We see a chapel and a basilica and hostels and colonnades—and suddenly we will have a new shrine." He smiled. "We may love our old shoes. But when we grow they do not fit. Fátima is always growing. I miss the old ways, but I cannot be selfish."

"Ti Marto, for many people the children's prayers to Our Lady brought miraculous answers. Do you know if anyone in your family or Lucy's had such an answer?"

He was silent for a minute. The rain fell steadily on the cabbage plants outside, on the corncobs laid out hopefully to dry on the pine needles.

"I remember two things, but it is not for me to call them miracles.

"The first thing was the day of October thirteenth, 1917. The day of the apparition. It seemed as if the whole world had come to our house, the one across the road there. So many people. And it was pouring like today. They did not change their shoes, of course. They tramped in mud and water. They stood on our chairs and our tables, even our beds. The house was full of dirt and water. You could not distinguish it from the road outside.

"So. We went, my Olympia and I, with the children to see the Miracle of the Sun. No one was left in the house or in the village. Everyone was at the Cova. But when we came back, the house was clean. Completely clean inside. We asked everyone, but no one did it for us."

He looked us full in the face. "To me and my Olympia that

was a miracle. It would have taken us a week to clean it. But it was clean.

"Then there was another thing. I have a niece, a very pretty girl. Her name is Virginia dos Santos. Her father, he is Antonio dos Santos Rosa. About four or five years after the apparition she was very badly burned. By the feet. She could not walk for many years. For a girl who cannot walk it is hard to get married. But finally her mother made a prayer and a promise to Our Lady of Fátima. And the girl was cured. Virginia is married now, and happy too."

Ti Marto seemed lost in reflection. In the half-light he looked like a fisherman patiently mending his nets, but his nets were not of rope but of prayer and of thought.

"Ti Marto, how does it feel to come so close to holiness? To have your own children chosen to see Our Lady?"

"God and Our Lady chose my children for the purpose of Fátima. They could have chosen any others." His shoulders shrugged. "It is a great grace. But it is not my merit that caused it. It is a great thing for me, but—I am still me. You understand?"

As he spoke we realized for the first time that mixed with the pride and wonder in his voice was the natural grief of a father who lost two children very young. Why do we forget that even the father of saints must yearn to have kept them close and seen them grow to maturity?

Over the whisper of the rain we could hear voices in the house jabbering at Tia Olympia, asking where her husband was. Ti Marto grinned with boyish pleasure.

"They will not think to look here! They do not know me

very well." He looked at us expectantly, awaiting the next question.

"Ti Marto, we are very young, just starting our family. We have three children——"

"Three? Ah!" He stopped us there, genuinely anxious to hear every detail about our little Marty and Michael, and Baby Catherine. Only after a long discussion could we go on:

"Look, we don't expect Our Lady to appear to them, or anything out of the ordinary at all. But we do want to teach them to serve God and to be good. You raised seven. You can tell us, what is the secret of a happy family life?"

The old man gazed into the twilight with the far-dreaming eyes of a sea captain.

"For me that is a very difficult question. This question of happiness." His hands moved slowly through the dusk, reaching for words. "For me my happiness is that never in my life have I known doubt. We have always been happy in the goodness of God, no matter what came.

"Happiness is not in greatness. Greatness is for the other life and not for this. Our happiness is only in God's mercy for us. Always I try to educate my children in the love of God and of Our Lady. The only happiness for the family is in prayer and in submission to God's will. That I know."

He paused in thought. "But happiness—ah, it is difficult today. Because of war. There is no charity in the world today. How can we be happy if we think of the other people . . . ?"

"You fought in a war once?"

"I was a soldier in the Portuguese colonies many, many years ago. It is the only time I have been away from Portugal or from this bit of mountains. I was born at the north end of

Fátima and today I live precisely the same distance from the parish church in this direction as I was born in the other direction. Not a very broad life, eh?"

"You worry about war and world conditions. Do you know anything about the United Nations and their work for peace?"

"I have heard of it."

"Will they bring us peace? Which way do you think we will find peace?"

"If the people say the rosary, peace will be. If they don't hear the word of Our Lady, there will be another war." Hands on his knees, he bent forward to make his point.

"Peace is easy. We need only to unite against evil. What more could we need to do?"

A dark-haired girl, his daughter-in-law, ran through the rain into the chicken coop, smiled at him, and busied herself tending the rabbits.

"Ti Marto," we asked, "one more question. You must know the secrets of prayer. Next to Our Lady, who is your favorite saint?"

"I have none. I pray to God, to Our Lady, and to Jesus Christ. The others are all the same thing, you know. My favorite prayer is the Our Father. It's *Our* Father, not *My* Father. So when I pray it, I pray for all."

The rabbits chewed quietly. A chicken meandered past our feet. The staunch little fig tree received the rain. The world of Ti Marto was at peace, patient under God's will. Some of that peace filtered into our own souls.

Suddenly he grinned. "You asked me about happiness," he said. "My Olympia and I have been married fifty-five years. And we are still sweethearts. We are a big joke around here, the way we carry on. Sometimes someone will say to me: 'Here, Ti Marto, here is a sweet.' And I say: 'Good, I will give it to my girl friend.' She still calls me her boy friend. Aha. One of these days, I always say, we will get married and settle down. But now we are still courting. Can you understand?"

We understood. Olympia today is toothless and pale and wrinkled. Once she was strong, a young widow with two children, and she caught Ti Marto's eye. To him, she has not changed.

"Have you more questions?"

"No, Ti Marto, we would not think of bothering you with more."

"It is no bother. It is one of the jobs God asks of me. You know Father De Marchi? When he was writing his book he asked me questions for months. Many months. Then he was through. I said: 'Father De Marchi, do you want to ask another question?' He said: 'No, you can die now. I am through.' He was joking, you understand, for he is my friend. So I joke too. When I saw him again, I said, 'Father, I am still alive!' And I teased him. Many times I remind him I am still alive. Then I thought, This is not good. I should not make fun of a priest. So I asked him to forgive me. He said there was nothing to forgive."

Ti Marto wrapped his arms around his chest and tickled himself in the ribs. "Hee-hee! So I say—I am still alive!"

"Ti Marto! Where is he? I want to see Ti Marto!"

A voice sounded imperiously across the wall.

"I do not know who that voice is, but if you are through I will talk to him. At least on Sundays the questions do not interfere with my work!"

Reluctantly we left the chicken coop. For the first time in an hour and a half we realized how wet our clothes were. The chill of late afternoon surrounded us. We set our faces to the rain and started up the muddy lane.

Chapter Thirteen

ARMY OF PEACE

The morning of the twelfth the sun shone gloriously.

The roads were clogged with black clumps of pilgrims, every one of them carrying a furled black umbrella. Whole families trudged along singing hymns, their food and clothes stowed in baskets on their heads. Burros plodded and skittered around the mountain bends, carrying children and their mothers and heavy saddlebags of provisions. Bicycle parties skimmed past. Cumbersome wagons, shared by two or three families, creaked and rattled on wooden wheels. In the stubble and rock on the wayside little groups were camping, some still sleeping, others cooking over tiny charcoal fires. Busses careened around fenceless turns, horns blasting. Cars of all vintages, ancient American models and shiny Jaguars and little Volkswagons, threaded their way through the obstacle course. It was one-way traffic to Fátima.

At each crossroad smartly uniformed police guided strangers along the route, past the ethereal cathedral of Batalha up into the stark hills.

At first glance Fátima itself resembled a disaster relief station until you saw the smiling faces and the rosaries and heard the hymns. By midmorning thirty thousand had arrived. Busses from the nearby railroad station disgorged their loads. Every room, every cot, every inch of camping space was taken, and still the crowds came.

We had been warned to make reservations to stay at the Consolata Seminary overnight. It would have been impossible to return to the Estalagem and back before morning, and it would have meant forgoing the all-night services at the shrine. In the driveway before the seminary stood chartered busses, two from Austria, one from Germany, and an array of private cars and taxis from Lisbon and Oporto. Seventy-two Irish policemen, polished and beaming, were just arriving for the pilgrimage. Shortly afterward, two weary and hungry teenagers from Germany roared up on their motorcycles.

The entrance hall was a genuine Babel. French, Italian, Spanish, German, Belgian, English, and Portuguese battered our ears. In the small religious-articles shop seminarians dauntlessly made change in and from ten different posted currencies and calculated postage rates to every part of the world. (Postage is a real confusion for Portuguese tourists, as there are two rates for postcards, depending on the length of the message. More than five words cost almost the same as a letter.)

We found our room large, light, airy, and monastically clean. The rooms in the Consolata Seminary are among the cheapest in Fátima and the best we had seen in our inspection

tour of available accommodations. We left our suitcase and
hurried over to the Chapel of the Apparitions. An Australian,
the genial Monsignor Leo Charlton, two Irishmen, and a priest
from India joined us. Holiday spirit perfumed the air. Smiles
were infectious, and your presence at Fátima was introduction
enough. Each new group arriving received jubilant welcome
from earlier comers. Being in Fátima that day was like being
part of a giant family reunion.

The chapel from a distance looked like a booth at a fair,
roofed over with green boughs and fresh pink flowers. The
square, once so desolate and vast, was abuzz with prayers and
greetings and song. Bands of fifty to a hundred pilgrims, ban-
ners floating high, marched slowly toward the Basilica, praying aloud in their own languages.

Near us two children and a man walked slowly down the
square supporting a middle-aged woman who was walking on
her knees. All four were reciting the rosary in calm voices,
oblivious of all around them.

We became aware of others traveling on their knees. Some
were alone, unsupported. One woman still balanced a basket
on her head as she made her way forward, lost in prayer. Some
held a blanket or padding, manipulating it carefully to protect
their legs. Others were barelegged and bleeding. It is more
than a third of a mile from the far end of the square to the
Basilica.

We went to buy bottles to fill with water from the spring
under the Sacred Heart statue. The bottles, encased in wicker,
are sold for a few cents by a curious-looking cripple in his
middle years at a booth set into the Old Hospital building.

"What about this water, is it supposed to be miraculous?" asked Monsignor Charlton.

"Not officially," said Hugh. "It is not even called holy water. Just Fátima water. You see, at the beginning, back in 1920 or so, there was no source of water here at all. There are no springs or streams for miles around, and the people simply collect rain water in cisterns, like the so-called well behind Lucy's house. But the Bishop——"

His words were broken off by a troop of German pilgrims marching past us singing hymns to Mary as they trudged toward the chapel.

"The Bishop worried about the pilgrims who had to bring their water with them. So when he bought this land to build a shrine he ordered the workers to dig a cistern for rain water. They began to dig right in front of the place where the Basilica was to be built. But as they dug, tiny streams of water sprang from under their picks. The cistern was soon full and brimming over with natural spring water. That was in November 1921. Today the water from that spring and from another found near it in 1927 are both gathered in a reservoir below the Sacred Heart statue. It never runs dry."

"You call that a miracle?" asked the Indian priest.

"Not for me to say. But I tell you this. Everyone knows there was no water here before. This ground doesn't hold a drop. Always dry except when it rains. And the pasture that was here was scrawny. Not like an oasis fed by underground waters, you see. But a miracle—who knows?"

We stood beneath the monument, waiting our turn at the faucets.

"Well, does the water do anyone any good? Doesn't look

very sanitary, y'know," said Monsignor Charlton. "Everyone seems to drink from those spigots as well as fill their bottles."

Hugh grinned. "Back in the twenties the government was very concerned about this water as a menace to public health. Sent delegates up here, wanted it covered up and destroyed. But they gave up. Maybe when they saw a few of the strange things that happen here—like pussing wounds disappearing when washed with it, or internal diseases going away. A lot of cases of cures are reported from this water."

"Miracles?"

"That word's not too popular at Fátima," said Hugh. "Call it what you will. It's a blessing to have water. And no one's yet gotten sick from it."

Our turn came. We had watched the begrimed coughing man ahead of us drink from the faucet. We looked at each other, remembering the tales we had heard of devout people in Lourdes drinking the spring water in which the sick had already been washed. Our stomachs were squeamish. We had been educated to believe in germs and viruses and microbes. But we had also been taught to believe in a God Who could overcome disease.

We drank the water. It did not taste very good, but it definitely did not infect us or make us sick. We filled our bottles.

We had an appointment to meet one of the permanent residents of Fátima, Dona Maria de Freitas. Late in the afternoon we pushed our way through the steadily growing throngs on the short main street of the Cova. We passed the little *pensão* with the amusing weather-beaten sign reading: "English Teas Spoken Here." Like every other, it was bulging at the front door. Women in saris mingled with teen-age boys in short pants from Germany in that smiling crowd. African faces, Chinese and Turkish, tall blond Scandinavians and a honeymoon couple from Switzerland—everyone was smiling.

Our destination was a small dignified white house at the far end of the street. A little marker inside the white stucco wall announced that this was the headquarters for the Blue Army, home of its international secretary. We knocked, and a sweet voice called for us to come in.

In a sunny room by the entrance we found Dona Maria by the bed of her invalid sister. The room was vivid and warm with life. A green-and-scarlet parrot strolled on the headboard, pecking at seeds on the sick woman's shoulder. Her dog, fuzzy brown, nestled at her feet. Songbirds fluttered in rambling, oversized wicker cages. As Dona Maria's mother is also an invalid, all her grown life, the tiny, springy-footed woman with the wide grin has tended sickbeds. Yet there is nothing of gloom or resignation about her or her sister.

Obviously they were used to company. The room was filled with guests when we arrived, a dark-skinned priest from Goa, a nurse from Germany, and a delegation of the Irish police. All wore small blue pins in their lapels.

"You have come to hear about the Blue Army too?" Dona Maria asked. "But you should know all about it. As I was telling these people, it was started by an American, you know, a priest in Plainfield, New Jersey. Father Harold Colgan.

"He, too, was very sick once. In November 1946, it was, he was taken to the hospital with a serious heart attack. They thought he might die or, at the best, spend all his days in bed. On December eighth, the day of the Immaculate Conception, he made what you Americans call a deal with Our Lady of Fátima. He promised to promote her cause to the fullest of his ability. He asked to receive good health.

"Almost instantly Father Colgan was cured. He went back to St. Mary's Church and began preaching. He got a parish group to sign pledges for the first Saturday devotions and the Fátima prayers. He called it a Blue Army of Our Lady to fight the Red Army of Communism.

"It spread almost overnight, without his effort at all. He never meant to go beyond his own parish. But poof!—it grew. Today we have four million members in twenty-eight countries!"

"What do you have to do to join?"

"You sign a pledge to say in reparation to the Immaculate Heart a part of the rosary every day, pondering on the mysteries. To fulfill the daily duties of your state in life. And to renew the pledge in moments of temptation. And you wear something blue to remind you. A blue pin, a ribbon, or a cord. It is very simple."

"In our country we have many Crusaders of the Blue Army," put in the German girl. "One of our handsomest young baritones, Alfons Holte, has organized hundreds of youth groups to say the rosary and pray for peace. For us that is a new kind of army!"

"And this little house is the headquarters at Fátima?" asked the Indian priest.

"Not for long." Dona Maria laughed. "We are building an International House for pilgrims behind the Basilica. The main altar will be designed according to the Russian rite, and the chapel will have a large dome, almost a replica of the domes of the Kremlin. And we have a Russian priest as a chaplain."

"Did you ever meet Lucy?" we asked.

"Only once. The time she came back to see her home and the Cova, just before she entered the Carmel. I shall never forget her smile. You cannot describe it. It is heavenly, I suppose. I spoke to her, to tell her I had known her mother well.

"I remember she stopped by the well behind her house, and she was thirsty. Someone went to get her a dipper, but she did not want one. She took a cabbage leaf from the garden and used it as a scoop, just as she had done as a child. She was almost gleeful about it."

Twilight was pressing on the windowpanes above the invalid's bed as Dona Maria summoned herself back from her memories. Briskly she rose.

"Here is a pin of the Blue Army. Wear it, and pray. And keep peace in your heart. For it is only from the heart of each one of us that God's peace can spread across the world."

Chapter Fourteen

CANDLES IN THE DARKNESS

Rain began to fall with the night.

Every bed in town, every inch of floor space, every nook of outdoor shelter was in use. Tents were pitched in the fields; squares of canvas tied to trees served as roofs. One trailer stood behind the butcher store, and at least twelve people were using it. The sanctuary, the hospitals and seminaries and convents, the hospices and *pensãos* were full. Under the half-built colonnades, along each wall and step of a building, families were staking their claims for the night. The air was sharp and chill.

Along the road campfires flickered. Peddlers offered cups of steaming tea and soup, savory bits of codfish and of cheese for sale.

We ate as usual at the Dominican convent, the one place in

Fátima where the food is designed for foreign stomachs. The Dominicans serve meals and rent rooms to women and to married couples and even accommodate children. On our arrival we had learned the password for Americans. You go to the convent at the foot of the hill below the seminary and ring the formidable bell at the door and ask for Sister Hyacinth. She is the only English-speaking nun there.

A brisk woman from St. Louis, Sister Hyacinth will take you in hand. She will explain how she cajoled the convent into providing a cuisine without oil, even going into the kitchen personally to teach them how to cook. She had not been home to the States, except for a brief visit a few years ago, in more than twenty-five years, but she is an alert and expertly informed companion.

Ordinarily the dining room is used only by the average daily influx of foreign pilgrims and by festive tables of wedding guests. Portuguese brides delight in being married at Fátima, and, for that matter, Portuguese mothers, in spite of all official discouragements, endure the worst difficulties to have their babies born in the shadow of the shrine.

On this night of the thirteenth we were grateful that Sister Hyacinth had made reservations for us. The large dining room was filled four times over. Pleasant-faced Portuguese lay sisters scurried from kitchen to table and back, balancing five-course dinners and the inevitable bottles of table wine. Somehow they remained serene. At our table we found a WAC sergeant who had saved up leave from her post in Germany just to come here for the thirteenth. Around us Brazilians, Africans, Ceylonese, Irish, and Portuguese hurried through their meal with a festive air.

It was nearly time for the candlelight procession.

We are not fond of crowds or popular demonstrations. We do not go to parades. We shrink from public rallies. Yet we found ourselves yearning to join in this procession to do honor to Our Lady. We bought the typical tall two-cent candles and the flimsy printed blue paper shades to shield them from the wind. With raincoats, sweaters, and rubbers we went to the Cova.

The wind was crying for vengeance, but the rain had nearly ceased. The square was thronged with black umbrellas. The Basilica itself was flooded with light, spilling over the white spire, gleaming on the gold crown at its peak. On the marble steps stood a large open-air altar protected by red draperies swaying with uncanny life in the gale.

The Basilica clock struck ten, and the procession began, counterclockwise around the square.

Only out of politeness could you call this a procession. It has no ordered path such as at Lourdes. Spontaneous and child-like, it grows in exuberance. As you stand watching, with your candle in your hands, the vast sea of flames that fills the Cova gradually takes shape before you. Thousands upon thousands of wind-tossed lights fall into line, twisting and turning to fit the cramped area of the square.

Over a loud-speaker a strong male voice led in the first of the special pilgrim songs:

> *"Avé! Avé! Avé! Mãe celestial,*
> *Avé! Avé! Avé, canta Portugal."*

And the dearly popular, seventeen-verse retelling of the story of the thirteenth of May rings loud and clear:

> *"A treze de Maio, na Cova da Iria,*
> *Apareçeu brilhando a Virgem, Maria.*
> *Avé, Avé, Avé Maria."*

For near an hour in the storm and the wind and the damp we sang and prayed, our candles guttering and flaring in the night. The Christopher's phrase rang through our heads: "Better to light one candle than to curse the darkness."

The darkness of that night was overpowering, but every soul in the Cova had lit a candle. The glow of thousands of tapers of faith overcomes the night.

We struggled to keep our candles alive, and when the wind whipped through the charred shades and blew them out, we lit them again. We knew that in our hands was a symbol of the answer to peace, a symbol that grew infinitely precious in the Cova on the eve of October 13. To this day we keep the blackened crumpled remains of the paper shades, mute reminders that we have promised to keep the flame alive in our hearts.

The procession was over, but no one left the square. In prayer and litany and ancient chant the praise of God continued.

At midnight the priest at the loud-speaker began the rosary in Portuguese:

"Avé Maria, cheia de graça, O Senhor é convosco! Bemdita sois vós entre as mulheres, e bemdito é o fruto do vosso ventre, Jesus!"

On the altar the Blessed Sacrament shone from the gold monstrance.

Decade by decade the voice announced the mysteries of the rosary and explained their meaning. He proclaimed the intentions for which thousands prayed that night in Fátima: for peace, for the conversion of Russia, for the sick, for the Church and the Pope, for the secret prayers of all pilgrims, for Portugal. And again and always, for peace.

Portuguese voices answered in the prayers of the rosary:

"Santa Maria, Mãe de Deus, rogai por nos pecadores agora e na hora da nossa morte."

Silently we prayed in unison, "Holy Mary Mother of God, pray for us sinners now and in the hour of our death."

It was after one. The priest at the loud-speaker informed us that throughout the night hours of prayer would be conducted for each of the groups of pilgrims in their own language. English prayers at two. German at three. Spanish at three-thirty . . . A constant stream of supplication and thanksgiving to God the Father.

The rain returned. The Blessed Sacrament was moved again into the Basilica. The crowd thinned. Some went to the all-night confessionals, or into the Basilica or the chapel to pray. A few went to rest.

We heard Hugh's voice: "Would you like to come over to the New Hospital? It might be interesting."

We followed him through the dark. All along our way whole families slept in the uncertain shelter of scaffolds and walls and archways and steps. They huddled under shawls and blankets, oblivious of us as we picked our way around them.

We stopped for a last look.

Around the streaming yellow light of the little chapel several hundred men and women knelt in the rain, shielding their candles with their bodies. Otherwise the square was dark. And full above it, gleaming white and gold, the brave, crowned spire of the Basilica pierced the night. The angels carved on the sides of that spire gazed upward as if confident of the light they could not see.

Chapter Fifteen

WONDERS AND SIGNS

The hospital was dark and creaking. The halls were lined with sleeping people, not patients but pilgrims, grateful for shelter from the rain. In the shadows a woman was nursing her baby. Four children slept entwined under a red wool blanket. An old man was snoring. The air was heavy with the odor of wet clothes.

An American pilgrimage of the sick had already been installed in their rooms and were asleep. There was nothing we could do to help, but some of the nurses welcomed our company. They were part of the band of Servitas who come to Fátima regularly to each pilgrimage to assist in whatever way they can.

"Have you ever seen a cure at Fátima?" we asked.

All four of them had. Their faces gleamed with eagerness. One, a pert little Englishwoman, told us:

"I was the nurse assigned to a woman who was one of the worst cases I ever saw. She had an open wound in her side deep enough to put your whole hand in. I sat up with her the entire night of the twelfth. She was delirious with pain and fever, often unconscious. I changed the dressing and cleaned the wound as best I could. The doctor examined her in the morning and called for a priest to give her Last Rites.

"The doctor did not think she should be moved to the Basilica for the Blessing of the Sick on the thirteenth. But she had come here only for that. We went personally and asked the Bishop's permission and carried her over on a stretcher. She was completely unconscious until the moment when the Blessed Sacrament paused in blessing before her. I was kneeling beside her. I confess, I was weeping.

"Suddenly she stirred. She opened her eyes and smiled, and sat up.

"I swear to you that when we examined her the hole in her side was gone. Closed completely. The dressings I had put into it lay outside on top of new skin. This all happened in the hour between the time we carried her to the Basilica and back to the hospital for the doctors to see her.

"She walked back to the Cova that afternoon to give thanks."

The crisp accent of England gave way before the tears of the nurse's emotion.

"Are you sure that happened?" The question was rude, but necessary.

"The whole report is in the Fátima files, attested by a medical commission. And the girl herself comes here almost every thirteenth to help the sick. There are many such *miraculadas* among our nurses."

Only the rain and the snores and rustles of the sleeping pilgrims in the halls penetrated the silence of that room.

"Are there many such miracles?"

"Many. One of the most moving occurred in 1937. There was a girl born sick. She had her first operation in 1917 when she was three *days* old, for a mastoid infection. She lost the sight of both eyes and the hearing in her left ear. She had two wounds left by one of her sixteen mastoidectomies, which had never healed. Pus came out of her nose and her wounds. In 1936 she contracted meningitis, and she had been paralyzed in a spastic position with a violently arched back, shoulders and neck drawn sharply back. She was that way for a year and a half. She bled terribly from her wounds. When she was brought here she was unconscious until the moment of the blessing.

"With help she walked back to the hospital. Doctors examined her at once. They found all infection and all paralysis gone. The wounds on the side of her head and in back of her ear had healed completely. I myself have read the records in the Lisbon Hospital of São José, where she had been until that October thirteenth, and to which she returned to convince the doctors of her cure. She, too, is here often as a Servita."

"Miracles happen here all the time. I have seen easily fifty myself. But they are not talked of much," said another nurse, a Portuguese woman.

"Why not? Don't most people come here seeking cures, like at Lourdes?"

"Oh no. Very few come here to be cured in proportion to the well who come to pray for peace and to give thanks to heaven. Our Lady is indeed worthy of her title, Health of the Sick, but Fátima is not a shrine of healing."

A very young nurse from Oporto laughed. "When they come in weather like this all they're asking for is pneumonia!"

"But no one ever caught a cold at Fátima!" said the English-woman.

We laughed. "No one?"

"Do you usually go around in wet clothes in unheated houses back in America? But look at you now."

We had to agree. We were drenched as we had been almost every day since our arrival, yet we were as well as we had ever been before.

"About the sick," said the Oporto nurse. "All of them are registered here at the Bureau dos Constations Medicales if they come to the hospital. In one two-year period we registered over five thousand cases. Among those, 260 cures were officially attested as beyond the realm of nature. Cases of cancer, of TB, of meningitis, Pott's disease, and so on.

"But healings are only a small part of Fátima. The more important miracles are those you cannot see. The inside ones," she said. "Like the people who have never been to confession in twenty or thirty years, and repent here. I've seen men come with their chins all bristling with defiance and heard them mock the wives who brought them here. Heard them insist they'll never pray. And then they do. Perhaps men like Fátima because here they find the rock of faith, stripped bare of nonessentials.

"I have seen skeptics who came to jeer fall on their knees in the mud and pray without embarrassment. In the lines before the confessional they wait four or five hours for their turn to make peace with God."

"Miracles, you say?" added the Englishwoman wryly. "Look at the pilgrims. There are many men among them. Usually at Mass or at special services at home you see women, not men. But at Fátima the young men and the old both come because they want to."

We had seen that to be true. Fátima is the one place of holiness where men are never outnumbered.

"If you stay long enough, give Our Lady half a chance at you, you cannot resist her," said the Englishwoman. "Did you hear the story about the photographer?"

"No."

"He was an American, from which publication I would not think it right to say. He came here with all his fancy equipment and his helper to do a story. But what he had in mind was an exposé, a sort of satire in black and white.

"He took pictures of everything that is unattractive and everything that would look ludicrous to outsiders. We have many ridiculous-seeming things here as there are everywhere that human beings gather. He shot them all. The little girls dressed in pink angel's costumes with wings, or robed as little versions of Our Lady. It does look funny, especially when some of the women dress up too. I once saw a 'Madonna' of fifty-five with her four grandchildren 'Madonnas' all tricked out with gold crowns and halos." The nurse giggled at the memory. "The thing is that they are a small part of a great whole. Isolated, they are fantastic. But to us they are not important."

Together they told the rest of the story.

The photographer made a public nuisance of himself. He seized on every objectionable detail of Fátima life. Some of the Portuguese, when they have received an answer to prayer, like to buy appropriate life-size wax images to lay on the altar as public acknowledgment of the favor granted. A wax baby, perhaps, or a leg for a cripple's cure. On special feasts you can see vendors carrying armloads of these figures, looking as if they were ghouls or grave robbers making off with their prey. A photo out of context would make excellent satire on any faith.

The photographer scorned the usual shots of devout prayer or of reverent pilgrims. For six days he roamed Fátima to depict the most loathsome cases of sickness and the most flagrant examples of the poverty of the people. Finally he even sent his friend to climb the Sacred Heart monument in the square and took a picture of him up there waving his hat.

The people of Fátima complained to the Bishop of Leiria, asking him to restrain the photographer. To their disgust, he refused to interfere.

On the day of the big pilgrimage the photographer installed himself in the Basilica for Mass. He took pictures of the Bishop from the worst possible angles, revealing and emphasizing his deformity. The Bishop paid no heed. He ran around the church during Mass, flash bulbs popping. He stepped over and on kneeling people and pranced around the side altars, clicking away with a grin.

Four separate delegations pleaded with the Bishop to have him thrown out of the Basilica. The Bishop refused.

At the most solemn moment of the Mass, the Consecration,

the priest raised the Host for all to see and adore. At that precise instant the stillness of the Basilica was torn apart by a groan from the depths of an agonized soul. With a wild cry the photographer dropped his camera and fell to his knees, hiding his face against the stone floor.

"He asked for a priest. Today he is a Catholic. He has been back here many times," said the nurse. "I guess the Bishop knew what he was doing when he refused to interfere. Our Lady can handle people better than any of us."

"The finest person I know in Fátima," said the Englishwoman, "is a man who was not cured. You must have met him. John the Cripple, or John da Capelinha, as some of us call him. He sells the bottles for holy water."

We remembered the spider-legged little man with a twinkling smile.

"John's mother's real name was Maria dos Santos Carreira. She died only a few years ago. But she was always called Maria da Capelinha, which means Mary of the Chapel. She was one of the first people to believe the children's tale of Our Lady and she was responsible for the first crude attempts at decorating the hallowed spot with bows tied to the trees and lanterns strung around. In a way she really built the Chapel of the Apparitions.

"On June thirteenth, 1917, when even the children's families had gone to celebrate St. Anthony's feast, Maria da Capelinha decided to follow Lucy and the others to the Cova to see what she could see. Of all her children, only the little cripple, John, would forgo the *festa* to go with her. They were firmly convinced after what they saw at the Cova.

"The next month, on July thirteenth, at Maria da Capelinha's request, Lucy asked Our Lady to cure the little cripple. And Our Lady said 'No.' She said that John's legs would never be straightened and that he would always be poor, but never in want. And she told him to be sure to say the daily rosary with his family.

"John was not cured. And he is still poor. But he is the happiest man you could hope to meet. He sells the bottles for a modest price. He is sacristan of the chapel, which had been his mother's lifework. And you should see him swinging along at a fast pace with his stick to help him. Everywhere he goes he is followed by white doves. They wait for him outside the church or his shop. They sit with him and play with him.

"He is not a 'cure.' But he is what Fátima is all about really. Accepting the will of heaven, being happy not in spite of but because of your troubles. He helps me just by being so happy. Do you know what I mean?"

One of the other nurses looked at us and said simply, "A cure is a nice bit of propaganda that God indulges in now and then, I like to think. They're like a fancy dessert. But the real meat of the business is not in signs and wonders but in the quiet sustenance of our souls."

"You remember," added the Portuguese girl, "that Our Lady asked Jacinta to suffer to convert sinners. She did not cure Jacinta. But she taught her to look on pain as a precious treasure—and that is a grace worth more than any cure."

From the hallway came the sound of a child talking in its sleep and a warm, mothering voice calming it. The nurses looked at their watches. It was nearly three in the morning, almost time for the special dawn Mass for the Servitas and the helpers of the sick.

We thought of our beds at the seminary and we were very tired. Wrapped against the rain, we went out into the night.

The voices of prayer sounded faintly from the floodlit square.

Chapter Sixteen

PILGRIM VIRGIN

"Did you ever hear about Our Lady's doves?"

We were sitting around the plain wooden tables in the seminary refectory. We had no food, but at three-thirty in the chill dark we were enjoying a last cigarette before bed. The white-haired priest across from us had confirmed the tale about John da Capelinha and his birds.

"You remember, of course," he continued, "that the dove is the symbol of the Holy Ghost. When Our Lord was baptized, the Holy Ghost came down in the form of a dove over His head as He stood in the River Jordan. And the dove today is the symbol of peace—whether it is Picasso's travesty or our own with the olive branch. That is just a footnote, mind you, an interesting side light on a true story. Make what you want out of it.

"Well. In December 1946, Portugal celebrated the tercentenary of its formal dedication to Our Lady. For the occasion the people decided to bring the statue of Our Lady from the chapel here at Fátima to Lisbon in a procession.

"Now the people of Portugal know as well as you or I that the statue is just plain wood. They're not idol worshipers. For them it's sort of like a banner, or a photograph, something that you can see and touch, a symbol of what you can't see and can't touch. They love that statue dearly because it reminds them of the Lady they love.

"So in honor to her they decided to carry it all the way to Lisbon on the backs of relays of men. The statue left the Cova on November twenty-second, on a large flower-covered platform. On December first the procession reached the town of Bombarral. There a good lady, Dona Maria Emilia Martins Coimbra, had purchased five white doves which she planned to release just as the statue passed, as a pretty way of paying homage. The birds were set free. Two flew away, as was to be expected. But three of the white doves flew down and landed at Our Lady's feet. All around them the crowds were singing and cheering and making the kind of confusion that drives most sensible birds away. But those birds stayed, even when people tried to shoo them away for fear they might soil the statue.

"They stayed for five days and five nights, never leaving it till the statue reached Lisbon. They did not eat and they did not drink. They fluttered and swayed and gently pushed each other around, but they did not leave the pedestal. Brass bands played. The statue was carried from town to town all the way to the capital. Searchlights and torches and rockets and fireworks welcomed the statue. Flowers and petals were thrown at it. The doves stayed put.

"Even when people tried to drive them away before taking the statue into that handsome new church of Our Lady of Fátima at Lisbon, the birds refused to desert. They kept vigil all through the night until the Solemn High Mass in the morning. For that time only did they fly away. And then, during the distribution of Communion, two soared and hid in the ceiling of the church, and the third stood with wings outspread on the crown of Our Lady's head.

"All three doves escorted the statue from that church in the candlelight procession through the streets later to the Old Sé, the Cathedral, and remained with it through the night until the Mass of the Immaculate Conception the morning of December eighth. And they returned with the statue to Fátima."

We studied the old priest's face.

"You needn't take my word. Look in the newspapers of 1946, you'll read all about it. And see pictures of it. It happened all right. And what it means is up to you. As for me, I must sleep now. My Mass is at six."

There was no sign of dawn. It was nearly four, but the rain only made the night darker. The refectory was chill, and the wooden seats were hard. Out of the shadows another voice spoke.

"That was the statue's first trip. But Our Lady of Fátima statues are traveling all over the world."

"The Pilgrim Virgin?"

"That's what they call the statues. Again it's a symbol, an idea of letting Our Lady visit where she is most needed, passed from house to house and country to country in a chain of reawakened devotion to God. It's really amazing what has happened." He leaned forward, and we could see his high forehead and shining blond hair above his clerical collar.

"Thirty years Our Lord lived a hidden life in Nazareth before He began His public teaching. Thirty years Our Lady of Fátima remained in Portugal, and then in 1947 she went out into the world. In May of that year thirty-five thousand delegates from all over the globe met in a Catholic Action Congress at Fátima and resolved to carry the statue in procession through all of Europe, as far as the Iron Curtain.

"From Portugal into Spain, through France into Belgium the statue was carried, and a train of reported cures and miracles marked its path. I myself am Belgian. I have seen what happened in Charleroi, where the Communists were very powerful. The statue came, and people were so moved that priests were hearing confessions in the streets because the churches were so crowded with souls returning to the faith they had discarded. Almost sixty thousand Communions in one day we had in Charleroi. It is as if Our Lady is willing to accompany her symbol and bless the hearts who welcome her and her Son.

"Another statue came to Canada and the United States. One to Africa, to Mombasa, south to the blacks and whites in the race-rioting city of Durban, to Rhodesia, Uganda, Angola, Mozambique, and Morocco. Everywhere people of all faiths welcomed it. Protestant and Moslem leaders greeted it officially. Moslem hymns echoed louder than the chants of the few Catholics in Africa. In Heliopolis, Egypt, where the Holy Family took refuge from King Herod's persecution, Our Lady of Fátima was warmly received.

"Moslems love Our Lady too, you know. That is the one, point on which our two faiths agree. Mary, the mother of Jesus, is a saint in the Koran, and they respect us for honoring her too. In one city in Arabia the Pilgrim Virgin procession for the sake of internal peace was directed to by-pass the Moslem quarter and stay within the English-speaking zone. But the Moslems rioted till the statue was brought to them too, and they did her greater honor than the Christians!

"Hardly a country in the world has not been visited by the statue of the Lady of Peace. Even in Moscow, not far from the Kremlin itself, a statue of Our Lady of Fátima is enthroned on an altar.

"People of every language, of every color and faith, are praying God that the world may be worthy, and Mary's promise of peace may come true."

Another man, a Scotch layman come to Fátima for the thirteenth, leaned forward. "Have you ever studied the dates of Fátima—and Russia?"

We confessed we had not.

"I'm not much on history myself, but look here!" He pulled out paper and pencil and wrote rapidly.

"*May 13, 1917, Moscow*. First terrorism directed by Lenin, the invasion of a church; children in catechism class trampled by horses. Blessed Sacrament defiled.

"*May 13, 1917, Rome*. Eugenio Pacelli, now known as Pope Pius XII, consecrated Bishop.

"*May 13, 1917, Fátima*. First apparition of Our Lady."

He tapped the page with his pencil. "From here on they are not so startling, these dates, but they are still interesting.

"On October 12, 1917, Germany pushed forward to control

143

the whole Baltic area, and Russia feared for her life. In the confusion on October 13, 1917, the leaders of Communism designed the second revolution which on November seventh was to sweep from Petrograd through all of Russia.

"And here in the Cova da Iria on October thirteenth—the Miracle of the Sun.

"From that moment on the power of Russia grew steadily through the twenties, when the Church was still investigating the truth of Fátima. On July 13, 1936, the anniversary of the revelation of the promise of Russia's conversion, came the first open act of revolt in what is called the Spanish Civil War, the tryout for the Communist battle forces. In that month the Russian Trade Unions sent more than £450,000 to aid the Republican forces.

"That war was fought next door to Portugal. It had been part of the published Communist plan to involve the whole Iberian peninsula. But the bishops of Portugal prayed to Our Lady of Fátima to rescue their country from the menace of Communism and the horrors of war. And, of course, she did.

"Skipping down through the years we come to Korea, another Communist testing ground. It was on May 1, 1948, that the 'People's Republic' of North Korea was inaugurated, May Day—and Mary's Day. The Communist day of rallies, and the start of the month of prayer to God through His mother.

"Two years later the war broke out, June 1950. Three years it dragged on with no hope of truce. In Holy Week, 1953, a Pilgrim Virgin statue consecrated at Fátima was sent to Korea at the request of some chaplains. She bore the title: Pilgrim Virgin of the U. N. Forces, Queen of the First Marine Division. And Thursday of the week of her arrival, the Communists gave their first evidence of wanting an armistice. That summer we had peace, for a time at least."

A wind rattled the refectory door. The rain in the cloistered porchway sounded cold. But our shivers came not from the rain.

A Consolata priest, Father Peter Mongiano, brother of Father Aldo, bent toward us with his intense brown eyes. "When your American Bishop Sheen came to Fátima for the big Holy Year celebration, he talked here in our chapel. He had been so impressed by the sight of the square at the closing procession of the thirteenth, where everyone waves his handkerchief in farewell to the statue as it is carried back to the Capelinha. He called it 'the white square of Fátima,' and he said it would defeat the Red Square of Moscow. He said: 'Communism is already defeated. It is only that the news has not yet leaked out.'"

Our friend with the page of dates cleared his throat. "Isn't it interesting to note that if the reports that came from the Kremlin are accurate, Stalin was stricken with his last illness on March 2, 1953, three days before he died. And March 2, as you know, is the anniversary of Pope Pius XII's election, and also his birthday. He is not idly called the leading man fighting Communism today."

"Where else has the Fátima devotion spread?"

"Portugal has ringed the Communist world with Fátima shrines. In each of her possessions on the peak of the highest spot in the country stands a Fátima statue facing Russia."

"Has anyone organized one all-embracing crusade to spread Fátima?"

"There are many organizations. Some specifically designed

to promote this devotion. Many are American, like the Blue Army, and the Sodality for Reparation to the Immaculate Heart. Father Peyton's Rosary Crusade is devoted to Our Lady.

"And in Portugal we have several, like the Crusaders of Fátima, who put out the *Voice of Fátima* newspaper in many languages, edited from the Bishop's residence."

From a table in the corner he brought over several copies of a small four-page newspaper. As we thumbed through, photographs and headlines in black and red caught our eye: "Fátima Devotion in Malta." "Our Lady of Fátima Enthroned in Moscow." "The Exhumation of Francisco." "Jacinta and the Family Rosary." Here and there were messages set in bold black boxes. One we will never forget. It said in toto: "Fátima is a place of penance. You will be disappointed if you hope to find material comfort of any kind." That is an exaggeration, for one can find the necessary comforts of bed and board; only luxuries are absent. Yet those lines distill the spirit of this shrine, where materialism is never permitted a toehold, lest it grow to strangle the clarity and immediacy of faith.

"Here, read this!" With an air of high expectation he shoved a copy of the paper for February 13, 1952, under our noses. In it was a report of the speech made by Cardinal Tedeschini, the Pontifical Legate to Fátima, at the closing of Holy Year, on October 13, 1951.

We read the paragraph indicated by the work-gnarled thumb of the Scotsman. In it the *Voice of Fátima* quoted the Cardinal as describing certain visions seen by the Pope at four o'clock on the afternoons of October 30, 31, November 1 and 8, 1950.

"In the Vatican Gardens," the paper quoted Tedeschini as saying, "the Holy Father looked toward the sun and then before his eyes the prodigy which took place years earlier on this day and in this place was renewed. Who can fix his gaze on the sun surrounded by a halo? The Holy Father could during those four days; he saw the sun, under the touch of Mary, disturbed, convulsed, palpitating with life, transmit, in a display of celestial movement, silent but eloquent messages to the Vicar of Christ. Is not this Fátima removed to the Vatican? Is not this the Vatican transformed into Fátima?"

We laid the paper down. "Is this true?"

"No confirmation has come from the Vatican," said our friend. "But interestingly enough, when Canon Marques dos Santos returned here to report on the tours of the Pilgrim Virgin, he announced that the Pilgrim Virgin had been in Rome on the precise dates mentioned by the Cardinal as the dates of the Pope's visions."

The gruff voice of the Belgian broke in: "Such things are impressive, if true. But what matters is that each individual should see the miracle of Fátima in his heart. It's the individual who counts. Each soul. Tomorrow you will see what Fátima can mean to an individual."

But tomorrow was already today. We had two hours to sleep.

Chapter Seventeen

THE THIRTEENTH

In the choir loft of the Consolata chapel seven altars stood, and at each one a priest was saying the Mass in low tones. Below, in the chapel itself, where more than two hundred people had sheltered all night from the storm, each altar was in use. Endless lines of the faithful came forward for Communion. Heel to heel with others facing other altars in the loft, we knelt to follow a Mass said by a priest from New Orleans, Father Marion F. Schutten.

Ordinarily seven o'clock Mass is also said in the open air of the square at the Cova while priests bearing ciboria each with six thousand Hosts make their way through the kneeling crowds, distributing Communion. But this particular day the rain forebade such proceedings, and we had decided not to attempt to find room in the Basilica. All over Fátima, in the

149

Chapel of the Apparitions, in the dim chapel of the sanctuary, in each religious house, Mass was being celebrated in every human accent.

We left the choir loft and our places were immediately taken by others. We hurried to the refectory for coffee and the heavy, half-damp Portuguese rolls which we had come to respect as being good for the teeth and definitely filling.

Thanks to the extraordinarily kind interest of the Bishop and Canon Galamba, we were given white arm bands to wear for the High Mass, which would enable us to stay close to the invalids during the Blessing of the Sick. On summer days that benediction takes place outdoors, but in inclement weather it is held inside the Basilica.

We had already read the regulations for pilgrims written by the Bishop of Leiria:

"The pilgrimages to Our Lady of Fátima must maintain their primitive spirit of piety, penance, and charity. . . . Always and everywhere, especially on the way here and at the Cova da Iria, the pilgrims must help each other, pray for one another, be courteous to one another, and in all ceremonies keep a respectful and deferential attitude.

"The sick, rich or poor, always hold the first place. Make room for them and help them whenever necessary. The walled enclosure must be considered a temple, at least during the duration of a pilgrimage. Keep silence, or, if necessary, speak low. . . . Lack of order is displeasing to God and disagreeable to most of the pilgrims."

With rubbers, raincoats, mufflers, and umbrellas we went to the square. Secretly we wondered if it might not be nearly deserted. Who but a fool would venture out in this weather?

The answer stood before us, a sea of black umbrellas covering thousands of souls who in their devotion were eager to be fools—"Fools for Christ," as St. Paul urges us to be.

We were late. Already the white statue of Our Lady, standing on a litter of white chrysanthemums, was being borne from the Chapel of the Apparitions. As the procession moved around the square, the refrain of the hymn sounded brilliantly through the rain:

"Avé, Avé, Avé, Mãe celestial!"

Their songs made the square a place of beauty. Their voices challenged the mountain winds and triumphed.

It was hard to believe that only a few miles away in Coimbra lived Lucy, from whose visions this devotion had sprung. Lucy has never witnessed one of these pilgrimages and probably never will, since she has chosen the contemplative life. We stood where the sheep had grazed and the lightning flashed, while in Coimbra Lucy still prayed.

Children in pink angels' wings, children dressed as Joseph or as the haloed Virgin, moved sedately through the crowds. A turkey gobbled and waddled along the colonnades, someone's dinner keeping fresh for later. And everywhere black umbrellas and the thin glorious voices of hearts who cherished a dream of a world of peace.

We climbed the steps of the Basilica to the red-draped altar. The arm bands won us each a spot of vantage.

We have never seen a Mass quite like this one.

The altar, high on a wooden platform, was surrounded by mud puddles more than an ankle deep. Construction of the colonnades had left the ground and pavement in sad shape.

The priests and bishops coming from the Basilica were forced to raise their robes and leap. We and the five or six hundred others who pressed close to the altar stood in two to three inches of water. Rain fell without mercy on the respectfully bared heads of the men. When we knelt, we knelt in mud.

But it did not matter.

Thirty-six years before, seventy thousand people had stood and knelt in the mud of this pasture, waiting for a miracle. For us the sun would not dance, but for us the simple prayers of the Mass, the Credo, the Pater Noster, were part of that miracle. Prayer is the road to peace.

Looking over that square, at the mud puddles and the soggy clothes, the discomfort and sacrifice which had gone into the journeys of these multitudes, we remembered the stories of the days when Jesus was on earth. Men and women, thousands of them, had followed Him far from home without thought of creature comfort to hear Him preach. And He had fed them from the few loaves and fishes and cared for their necessities. So in our own day He would feed us with the Bread of Life, and with truth and with faith, who had come apart from our homes to honor Him. His first miracle had been at Mary's request at the wedding feast of an embarrassed young couple. He has never ceased helping those His mother loves.

Mass ended, and quietly we found our way with the crowd into the Basilica.

That morning the church was not physically an inspiring sight. Rain dulled the stained glass. A scurf of mud and damp defiled the floor. It was crowded with officials and clergy and with the sick. Perhaps the place by the pool at Bethesda was not much cleaner when Jesus stopped there to heal the man who had no one to carry him into the healing waters. Was the house at Capernaum not crowded and travel-stained when they uncovered the roof to lower the one sick of the palsy to be healed by the Lord? The divine is no stranger to the confusion of crowds.

The sick were arranged in neat aisles, nurses, stretcher-bearers, and families beside them. They sat or lay in near silence, waiting. Those who were able prayed. Here was a Spanish girl with a monstrous large head, a pretty child of nine or ten. An American woman paralyzed on a stretcher. A Frenchman with a twisted leg. Tubercular cases. Cancer cases. The blind, the deaf and dumb, the halt, the epileptic. People whose lives were a prison of pain and a sanctuary of hope.

The Bishop, with his attendant priests, carried the Blessed Sacrament in a brilliant gold monstrance down from the altar. This is in Catholic eyes the undeniable real presence of Our Lord under the guise of the white wafer of the Host, what little Francisco had called "the hidden Jesus." The Bishop paused before each invalid separately, blessing them in the name of the Father and of the Son and of the Holy Ghost.

We saw no cures. But we saw something more moving, the peace that came to cool the faces of those in torment, the clear-eyed serenity of those who accepted the fact that they would not be healed.

There was the testimonial of faith: the souls who came to their Lord, knowing that He had the power to cure them, and who were refused and yet did not falter. Like St. Paul, who had prayed that this infirmity be taken from him and still accepted it as a safeguard against the sin of pride. Like Little

John da Capelinha, whose intellect may not equal St. Paul's, but who smiles as he swings along on his hobble stick and welcomes the doves with the dawn. Like the mother of this swollen-headed child who has brought her to Fátima every year of her life and who leaves the Basilica with peace in her eyes.

Peace! It is born in the hearts of those who accept both God's bounty and His inscrutable ways. It is nurtured in the houses of prayer—in cathedrals and parish churches, and in homes where prayers are said together. Only from the people, separately united in faith, can peace come to the world. And only from God can the people learn the secret of peace.

We followed the unhealed sick into the open air. It was one o'clock Daylight Time, noon by God's time, exact anniversary of the Miracle of the Sun.

The square seemed a fluttering sea of white. Thousands upon thousands of white handkerchiefs waved and waved in farewell to the statue as it was carried slowly back down to the Chapel of the Apparitions. It was an outburst of longing for the heavenly Lady they loved and could not see. From every throat rang the most famous and moving of Fátima hymns, the "Adeus":

> *"O Virgem do Rosário, da Fátima Senhora,*
> *De Portugal Rainha, dos homens protectora!*
> *O Fátima, adeus!*
> *Virgem Mãe, adeus!"*

This was the white square of Fátima which Bishop Sheen had seen as the symbol of defeat for the Red Square of Russia, this citadel of prayer and love unconquerable.

The rain had stopped. The sun, fresh and clear as spring-time, smiled overhead.

We stood blinking and confused until our eyes grew used to the light outside the Basilica. We pictured to ourselves the day like this one when that sun had seemed unleashed from the firmament, about to destroy the world with the same light that had once warmed it, prevented only at the last minute by the Hand of God. In our day men were facing destruction from a source as primordial as the sun, the fierce force of the atom. And only God, Who fashioned man and atom, can prevent that disaster. Perhaps there lies one meaning of the Miracle of the Sun.

But for us there was another, deeper, more personal meaning.

In that noontide at Fátima the clouds of halfheartedness which had dimmed our faith rolled back. The sun of God's love poured in on our souls, devastating and blinding as it burned away the vapors of fear and pride. Separately we faced our own souls and surrendered them with all their faults to God.

Not until months later would we find the words to tell each other of that moment, and even then the words were inadequate, faulty tools for the soul. For that brief time we had stood absolutely alone with God in those overwhelming throngs, and a miracle had come into our hearts.

Chapter Eighteen

COIMBRA

We were to see Lucy and talk with her.

Without exaggeration that piece of news left us numb. When she entered the Carmel in 1948, Lucy voluntarily cut herself off from the world to dedicate herself to prayer and meditation. Before that time, when she had lived as a Dorothean nun in Spain, she had been protected somewhat from tourists and sight-seers and the devoutly curious. Still, for thirty-one years she had been questioned and requestioned by investigators and historians and biographers and Church authorities. It is only human to allow her privacy now.

We knew that even high-ranking clergymen have trouble obtaining an interview with her in the Carmel. We would never have dared to ask such a favor. At luncheon with His Eminence, Cardinal Spellman, in New York before we left, we had agreed earnestly that such a thing would be impossible. Yet when we carried his letter of introduction to the Apostolic Pro-Nuncio in Lisbon, Monsignor Umberto Mozzoni, that volatile cultured man suddenly whirled on us with the question that stunned us:

"Would you like to see Lucy?"

Even then we had not believed that it would come to be. The final decision lay with the Archbishop of Coimbra, His Excellency, Dom Ernesto Sena de Oliveira, under whose care the Carmelite convent, and consequently Lucy, are placed.

We were told to appear at his office the day after the thirteenth.

We were four in the car setting off for Coimbra, including Father Aldo, who was to lend us moral support and his command of languages, and Martin's sister Mary, who had recently joined us at Fátima. We were curious to see Coimbra, if only as tourists. For nearly a year we had been teased about a song currently popular in the United States under the title, "April in Portugal." Not until we arrived in Portugal did we learn that the melody is actually a *fado,* a song of love and springtime in the city of Coimbra. Who could resist a visit there?

Coimbra is the home of one of the oldest universities in Europe, established there in 1306. Students still roam the narrow cobbled streets in black robes tattered with picturesque drama. It is the custom for a scholar to tear a piece from his robe as a token for his sweetheart, and the swains who pace the byways with books and guitars and voices raised in song are not at all single-hearted.

But Coimbra was old before the university. In Roman days

it flourished, and at Conimbriga, not far away, one can walk among the ruins of a mosaic villa built centuries ago, and tread the original stones of the highway that led to Rome. The Moslems favored Coimbra and made it theirs. The first king of Portugal lived here, and Coimbra was the capital city long before Lisbon. Here one can see the crystal tomb of Queen St. Isabel of Aragon and trace the steps of St. Anthony, who attended this university and lived in the little church now called Santo Antonio dos Olivais.

Today it is the home of Lucy of Fátima.

Time seems to have paused to rest beside the gallant Mondego River, merging past with future on its soft green banks.

We arrived at the Archbishop's Palace.

The man at the door solemnly requested us to go down the hall until we reached the stairs, and then turn left.

The hall was long. At the far end we glimpsed an ornate marble staircase leading up toward exquisitely landscaped fountains. Fortunately we were proceeding at a sedate pace. Were any stranger to violate decorum and run toward those stairs he would surely flatten his head against a stone wall. They are only an illusion, a *trompe-l'oeil* mural, the most effective we have ever seen.

The real stairs, a tall spiral, were further on to the left. We entered the Archbishop's anteroom, furnished with magnificent antiques and filled with callers awaiting their turn on diocesan business.

We were growing nervous. The Archbishop might very well ask us why we thought we were worthy of an interview with Lucy. For that we had no answer. We did not think we were.

He received us with a smile and a firm handclasp. He

did not like interpreters, he said. Surely we could speak French?

We nodded. Once indeed we had been able to speak French with American school accents but with some fluency. Yet to our horror our answers to the questions he phrased in perfect French emerged in Portuguese. For three weeks we had wrestled unsuccessfully with this new language. In this moment of minor crisis all other tongues had fled. Not even a *"Oui"* or a *"Non"* remained. Automatically we murmured *"Sim,"* and *"Não,"* and *"Obrigada"* instead of *"Merci."* It was a fiasco.

Archbishop Oliveira is a man of kindness. He took pity on our red faces and cut the interview short. No questions. Only the smile, and astonishingly the letter which would be our passport to visit Lucy.

Humbly we took our leave. Father Aldo remained behind, rejoining us in a moment with a grin and a shrug of his graceful shoulders.

"I shall not be going in with you. The Archbishop said to me: 'I am sorry, but I have no authority to permit you to visit her too. Perhaps you can offer it up as a penance, my son?' And so I shall take you there and arrange things for you and I shall wait outside."

We felt even more humble than before as we drove toward the Carmel.

We waited outside while Father Aldo carried our letter into the convent to be forwarded by a revolving dumbwaiter system to the Mother Superior. The answer came back:

"Could you return later this afternoon? We are about to begin our daily observance of three hours of complete silence."

We lunched in elegance of another era at the Astoria Hotel. We wandered through the town, peering into basket shops and inspecting the venerable twelfth-century cathedral. But our minds were fixed on the approaching hour of three.

We have encountered many newsworthy and some awe-inspiring personalities in our lives. Between us we have met a cross section ranging from presidents and poets to screen stars and murderers, and conducted ourselves like normal, poised human beings.

But meeting Lucy was something else again.

For one thing, Lucy's cousin Jacinta is known to have had the gift of reading souls. Among the many well-documented examples of this was the time when in her last illness she was taken to hear a sermon by a famous and eminently respected priest. Sadly she turned to the nun who accompanied her. "That priest will turn out badly, Mother, even though you would not think it now," she said. Inside a few months the same priest was excommunicated and lived in flagrant public scandal.

Jacinta had told her doctors of their private sins and foretold their deaths. Did Lucy share the same power of piercing the secrets of other hearts? She has never made that claim, yet the memory of her cousin is disturbing.

For another thing, what can you possibly say to one who has spoken to Our Lady? We had decided firmly that we would not ask her again the questions she had endured so patiently, so often. She has written her memoirs. Countless interviews with her have been published. We had read most of them.

"What did Our Lady look like?" She had answered that in her memoirs.

She was "all of white, more brilliant than the sun, dispensing light, clearer and more intense than a crystal cup full of crystalline water penetrated by the rays of the most glaring sun."

"What was Our Lady's expression?" Father Thomas McGlynn, the noted sculptor-priest, had asked her in 1947. In his book, *Vision of Fatima,* we had read the reply:

"Pleasing but sad; sweet but sad."

"She was all of light," Father McGlynn quoted Lucy as saying. "The light had various tones, yellow and white and various other colors. It was more intense and less intense. It was by the different tones and by the differences of intensity that one saw what was hand and what was mantle and what was face and what was tunic."

Only a year before, in 1946, William Thomas Walsh had talked with Lucy in an interview recorded in his book, *Our Lady of Fatima:*

"When the Angel . . . gave you Holy Communion at Cabeço did it seem to you like a dream or a vision, or was it like the reality of receiving Holy Communion in a church?"

"I cannot be absolutely sure of that," said Lucy, "because I was not in any ordinary state of mind during such an experience and there was something so intimate, so interior, so intense about the apparition of the Angel and what he said and did. But I believe it was like the real experience of receiving in a church for I felt the contact of the Host."

"Have you had any revelations from Our Lady about the end of the world?" he asked.

"I cannot answer that question."

Wisdom beyond that of a plain child of the mountains lay

in that simple answer. A yes or a no would have revealed something about the secret that rests with the Bishop of Leiria. The little girl of Aljustrel had grown into a woman of wisdom and poise.

From her memoirs and from the testimony of her companions at the Dorothean convent, we knew that Lucy was still no stranger to heaven. Our Lord Himself had spoken to her at least twice in the intervening years. Our Lady is still her intimately visible friend. Humble and unassuming Lucy is, silent about her experiences except when she details them in writing under obedience to a superior.

We could not probe beyond those revelations. But what could we say to such a woman? The only thing we really wanted was to ask her to pray for us, and even that seemed presumptuous.

We entered the convent in Coimbra with deep misgivings.

Chapter Nineteen

LUCY

The entrance hall was dark, windowless. A tiny wizened lay sister opened the door for us and bowed us into the chapel to wait. The chapel is the only part of the convent open to the public. It is large, light, and cheerful.

On a side altar stands the statue of Our Lady of Fátima which Lucy prefers to any other, much less ornate than those usually seen. The Virgin's hands are stretched outward, half in welcome, half in blessing. The Immaculate Heart, circled with thorns, is separated from the body of the statue, standing out in front of it as a symbol might stand in a vision. The face is infinitely tender.

Before us stood a statue of another Carmelite nun who had been blessed with visions of heaven, St. Teresa of Avila, spiritual mother of this order, and a saint dear to Lucy's heart.

Further forward to the right of the main altar and built into the wall was a wide tall panel of grillwork completely covered with metal spikes, each an inch wide and half a foot long—an unsettling sight for modern eyes. To someone with an incurably romantic mind, it might recall a medieval tale of star-crossed lovers, with a spurned swain casting himself to death against that wall. But the spikes, blunt-tipped, are no more than a symbol of the complete removal from the world which is the life these women have chosen.

Father Aldo led us to a corner of the chapel near the main altar to show us a small aperture in the wall.

"Through this the sisters one by one receive Holy Communion. This is as near as they get to the world we know."

He smiled at us speculatively. "You do not think much of this life, do you? But there are many mansions in the Father's house—room for everybody, a home for every kind of soul. Contemplation can mean freedom. Perhaps it is hard for you to understand?"

A murmur, a slight sibilance hummed through the chapel, yet we saw no one. Father Aldo pointed upward. At the back and sides far above head level, thick screens were built into the walls. Behind them unseen nuns were praying.

The little old portress ran on noiseless feet into the chapel, knelt quickly, then bobbed up to summon us with silently flapping arms. We left Father Aldo and followed her into the reception room.

It was bare as a schoolroom in summer. Two plain tables. Three wooden chairs. The focal point of the room was a grille of the same blunt iron spikes, spaced widely enough to permit conversation and a fair view. The chairs faced the grille. We sat down.

At first we could see only a dark space ahead of us. A gentle voice in flawless English, spoke.

"Mr. and Mrs. Armstrong? And Miss Mary Armstrong?"

"Yes." Gradually our eyes made out the figures of two nuns seated facing us. They wore black veils covering the top part of their faces down to the nose. It is not a normal part of their habit, and when they receive the clergy or their own families they do not wear it.

The voice belonged to the Mother Superior, Mother Mary in Christ, whose complete command of both languages was our mainstay.

Time, we knew, was scarce. Other sisters were having other guests this afternoon, long-awaited visits with relatives. We could not usurp the one reception room. What would we say? Our questions seemed desperately inadequate. But we were saved the first move. Mother Mary in Christ was already talking:

"You are writers, journalists? We have read about your books in the reviews and the newspapers."

"Yes, Mother."

"Lucy had already told me that she is very anxious to correct the impression the world has about her father. Certain books have painted him in a very bad light. Can you help her?"

"We will try."

We knew the stories about her father, Antonio dos Santos, whose nickname had been Abobora, the Pumpkin. The most polite version was that "he spent all his free time in the tavern," that he did not share the faith of the children or go to Mass, and that he was furious at all the commotion over the apparitions, revenging himself in beating Lucy. We had heard that he was irresponsible and a drunkard. People have a tendency to build up the goodness of one person by contrasting it with the evil of another, even if they have to exaggerate both to fit their fables.

Lucy did not intend to permit such a black-and-white treatment of the man she loved dearly. Eagerly and urgently she defended her father, while Mother Mary in Christ translated it into the version we print here.

"He was a good father," said Lucy. "He worked from morning to night, and gave every penny that we needed to his family. It is the custom on Sundays for the men to stop at the tavern after Mass to drink, and he joined his friends there.

"But he was not a drunkard.

"He not only worked his own property, but he worked for others too. He was an overseer for another landowner of consequence. That shows you, he had to be reliable and trustworthy and competent, doesn't it?

"There is a story that he sold our flock of sheep to drink up the money and leave us penniless after the apparitions.

"It is true the flock was sold. But not until after my father's death in 1918. I was the shepherdess of the family because I was the youngest of the seven. But so many people came to see me after the apparitions. They called me home from the fields to question me. They came any time they chose. And I had to answer them. So the flock was left alone, for the older girls had too much else to do to care for them. I could not take care of them properly, so my mother sold the flock.

"But every family has a flock of sheep. And then we had none. So the gossip made this story. My father died most suddenly. But his things were well in order. And he is not to blame for the sheep. If anyone is, I am.

"There is another story that my brother Manuel left home because he could not get along with my father. The story makes my father out to be a very mean man.

"This is not true at all. My brother Manuel stayed home on good terms with my father. He did not leave home until his marriage, after our father's death.

"The story comes from a mistake in identity, a very easy mistake to make. The one who left home was my cousin, a soldier, whose first name is the same as my real brother. His name is Manuel dos Santos Rosa.

"You see, Tia Olympia (mother of Jacinta and Francisco) was my father's sister. She was married twice, and her first husband (not Ti Marto) was my mother's brother. So Manuel dos Santos Rosa, who did leave his home, is my cousin and Jacinta's half brother, and he shares the name of both our families.

"My brother was Manuel dos Santos, who would not wish to be thought to have fought with my father. He left home to go to Brazil, and he went because an uncle of ours wanted him to live there in the state of São Paulo."

"He lives in Brazil still?" asked Martin.

"Yes."

"Then you have an American in the family too?"

When the question was translated, Lucy burst into laughter. Tenuous though the joke was, it delighted her. She kept repeating over and over:

169

"An American dos Santos! Imagine that!"

Her laugh was lovely, unself-conscious as a young child's, fresh as May. Her voice itself was strangely melodic and gentle. Portuguese is not by any standard a pretty language. It is more nasal than French, and many words end in heavy "sh" sounds. The voice must flatten to encompass its range.

But Lucy's Portuguese sounded soft and poetic and happy. Happiness exuded from her, melting away the grille and the spikes, reaching out toward us with a warmth of friendship. We had the feeling that she loved us, in the half-forgotten, biblical sense of loving your neighbors.

Our eyes had grown used to the gloom. We could see the lower part of her face clearly. She has always been described as plain and homely. Her photographs make her look almost ugly, quite possibly because shyness freezes the easy mobility of her face. But Lucy in life is far from ugly.

Her smile is a gift from heaven. Even in repose the smile rested on her lips, hopeful, confident as a bride's might be.

"Will you please try to correct those errors?" she asked.

We promised.

"Have you any specific questions for Sister Lucy?"

"Someone has asked us to ask you again whether the prophecy about Russia was actually made to you in 1917 and why it was not revealed then, when it would have been far more startling and effective."

Lucy smiled patiently. "The prophecy was made in July 1917. It was part of the secret. Our Lady specifically made us promise not to tell then. I have explained that in my memoirs."

There was no better answer for those who could not understand delay in reporting such a prophecy. "God did not wish me to be a prophetess," Lucy had written humbly in those memoirs. And God's ways are mysterious. Her tone seemed to imply that of all parts of the message of Fátima the prophecies were the least important.

"The first Saturday devotion is spreading rapidly. Even non-Catholics have heard of it in our country. And because of the message of Fátima they are very interested. Some of them have even asked Catholics to make the first Saturdays for them. Have you any message for them?"

"Ah! Poor things!" Lucy's voice was full of pity and love. "Our Lady must hear that prayer!"

"Have you any special message for the people of the United States?"

The Mother Superior, who had been interpreting without comment, listened to that question gravely, but she tittered just a little as she turned toward Lucy. We heard the flow of Portuguese and then an explosion of ill-concealed giggles. Struggling for solemnity, Lucy whispered her answer. Mother Superior translated.

"Lucy says: 'No. Our Lady had no special message for the people of the United States. She never mentioned your country at all.' "

They had misunderstood. Their laughter had meant only that they had believed we thought the United States important enough in heavenly plans to be part of the remaining secret, perhaps. They had little use for such a thought—and who could blame them?

"We meant, has Lucy herself any message we could bring to the people of the United States? There are many who would be grateful for any word at all."

Lucy considered for a long time.

"I have nothing to say that is very unusual or startling. And it will not be very popular or smart, I am afraid.

"When I think of the United States I think about this: One of the things Our Lady especially asked for was modesty in dress. There seems to me to be not much modesty in the life of the women of your country. But modesty would be a good sacrifice to offer to Our Lady, and it would please her.

"If the Catholics in your country could make a league for modesty in dress——"

We interrupted to tell Lucy that there were indeed such leagues. One we especially remembered was the group of high school girls who had convinced certain manufacturers that there was a large market for dance dresses that were pretty yet decent.

"Oh, try to implement that league!" exclaimed Lucy. "And it will greatly please Our Lady."

Strange that a woman who had spoken with heaven of the urgent realities of war and peace should pick out only the immodesty of American dress for comment! Yet this was no prudish old maid speaking. Lucy from childhood had loved to wear frills and furbelows. Her memoirs are rich with details of the gold chains and earrings, the beaded and feathered shawls she dressed in for the *festas*. Lucy was a gay child, with enough natural vanity to recall that:

"In my neighborhood no other girl was dressed as prettily. I think my sisters and my godmother, Teresa, were surprised to see that one so plain could look so nice. The other children would please me by crowding around to admire my pretty things."

Not a killjoy. Not a sanctimonious spinster, in spite of her dark plain conventual habit. Why single out fashion? Because Our Lady had asked for modesty in clothes. Because she had reminded the children that "the sins which cause most souls to go to hell are the sins of the flesh." Because dress that is immodest springs from an upside-down idea of sex, not as a pleasure approved and designed by God, but as an end in itself.

What Lucy was saying is simple. The wrong attitude toward sex can destroy the whole system of family life and all of morality. The family is the cradle of religion and of liberty. Attack the sanctity of marriage and you weaken the structure of faith and of democracy. Strengthen one family and you bulwark a nation against decay and destruction. One way, so incredibly simple, to serve God is to promote modesty, no matter how unpopular the idea may be.

"That would be a good *sacrifice* to offer Our Lady." Lucy knew the pangs of a clothes-conscious heart.

But that word "sacrifice" had led us to the one question we most wanted to ask.

"Over and over you have said that Our Lady asked for sacrifice and penance to atone to God for the world's offenses. What do you mean by penance? To our ears penance has a foreign, even medieval sound. It sounds like flagellation or hair shirts, or walking on bleeding knees as some people do at Fátima. Is that what Our Lady wants from us?"

"Our Lady asked two things above all, penance and prayer," said Lucy. "By penance Our Lady meant especially the penance imposed by the *exact* accomplishment of the duties of our daily life."

"Is that all?"

She smiled at our surprise. "That in itself is all God has ever asked of us. That we should fulfill our station in life, that all the tiny details are cheerfully done, and that our job should be done as perfectly as possible.

"Our first job is to keep God's laws, His commandments, perfectly. And then we must accept whatever tasks lie in our path and turn our daily duties into prayers, weave them into a rosary, by doing them in His service.

"For a father and mother it means bringing up their children to the best of their ability, working for them, caring for them, cleaning, cooking, scrubbing. When done with the spirit of doing them perfectly for His sake, it is penance. For children, their duty is to obey their parents and learn and grow as perfectly as possible.

"The very first sacrifice that God asks of anyone is to keep the straight way. It is a very simple request. But it is the hardest of all to fulfill."

Those words fell like a quiet sunburst into the dimness of that room. We who shrank from the unfashionable word "penance" had nevertheless been so stirred by Fátima that we would have been willing to attempt almost anything to meet Our Lady's requests. We had read of the penances the three children had inflicted on themselves. Under the uncompromising orders of the Bishop of Leiria, Lucy had described them in her memoirs. The three of them had imposed on themselves strict fasts and long thirsts. They had knotted rough ropes next to their skin and worn them night and day. They had taken on these discomforts willingly and with the approval of Our Lady. At her direction they had discontinued them when their health weakened. Taken in relation to a request for penance, that story is disturbing.

But now, in the gentle words of Lucy we had found that, like all the true mysteries of life, the secret of heaven was unutterably simple. Of Lucy and of all of us, God asks only one thing—that we love Him and serve Him in every moment of our lives, accepting His will and making it ours. The heroics of martyrdom are for the few whom He calls to assume them. But there is heroism and redemption in the smallest act done in His Name.

That in itself is penance, the inward turning away from all that offends God, and the daily pursuit of His will. Is it strange that penance and prayer could save the world?

"I am sorry, but our time is up. Another sister's guests are here, and we must leave now."

Lucy whispered in the Mother Superior's ear.

"Sister Lucy says she will be happy to pray for you and for all your intentions and for all who are dear to you."

"Thank you. But before you go we have a present for Lucy. There is in America a Christian brother, Brother Adrian Lewis of Manhattan College, who is famous for his artistry at etching holy pictures on leaves and petals. When he heard we were coming to Fátima he made a special one and asked us to deliver it to Lucy. It is a picture of the apparition."

We held the leaf close to the grille. Supple but dry, it is a green maple leaf about four inches wide. On it, in infinitely delicate fretwork, is engraved the Lady of Fátima and the three children, Lucy included, kneeling in aspiration toward her.

"Ah! It is too dark. I cannot see it well. Could you hold it up to the light from that window?"

As we held it up the veil fell back a bit from Lucy's face as she stared at the leaf. Her eyes, deep and dark, fastened on the leaf, and her smile was tremulous as bird song.

"It is beautiful! May I keep it?"

We promised to deliver it through the revolving dumb-waiter. There was no way to pass it through the grille.

"Thank you so much," said Lucy. "And thank Brother Adrian."

"Thank you, and good-by."

The grille closed. We looked around at the room and the tables and chairs. We felt as though we had been away from the world a long time.

Chapter Twenty

"FÁTIMA, ADEUS!"

We went back to Aljustrel in a day of jubilant sunshine.

We walked past the well, past Valinhos, to climb again to the Cabeço and kneel where the angel had knelt with Lucy and Francisco and Jacinta. The sun rested on that white rock like the Hand of God. Its brilliance shattered our hearts.

We said the prayer of the angel:

"My God, I believe, I adore, I hope, and I love You. I ask forgiveness for those who do not believe, nor adore, nor hope, nor love You."

We remembered the words the angel had spoken: "Pray in this way. The hearts of Jesus and Mary are ready to listen to you." And we knew they were listening, yearning to hear that prayer echoed from every corner of the world God had made.

177

Down through the fields we went for a farewell to Ti Marto and Tia Olympia, and up the road to the Cova.

Pilgrimage days were over, but some thirty people were kneeling at the Chapel of the Apparitions. The wind was rich with autumn glory as we began our rosary.

Faces rose before our eyes. The innocence of little children playing by the well. The twinkle of joy in the patient work-worn face of Ti Marto. The loving acceptance of the unhealed sick.

We left the chapel and walked toward the Basilica. On the steps sat John da Capelinha, covered from his hat to his mis-shapen legs with fluttering white doves. He rose and went toward his shop. The birds followed him like a blessing.

We stood before the main altar of the Basilica, flanked by the tombs of Jacinta and Francisco. The church was warm with sunshine and the prayers of black-shawled women. Around us the bronzes over each altar recalled the life of the little Jewish maiden who had brought Christ into the world. In front of us stood a statue of the Lady of the Rosary, who came to the sheep pasture begging the world to welcome God into their hearts.

Here was an appeal every heart can answer, regardless of creed. She asked that we remember the reality of sin and shrink from it. She asked that we pray and live as God wishes us to, obedient and loving as a little child. She promised peace. Peace in our lifetime in freedom from war. Peace after death in freedom from hell. Peace in our souls forever as a reward for loving our Father.

That was the essence of Fátima. We had read in Lucy's First Memoir:

"In this apparition [October 13] the words which were most engraved on my heart were those of our Heavenly Mother's request:

" 'Do not offend God any more, for He is already very much offended.'

"What a loving expression of grief, and what a tender request! Would that it might echo throughout the world, and that all the children of our Blessed Mother might hear her voice!"

Appendix One

HOW TO REACH FÁTIMA, and WHERE TO STAY

AIR TRANSPORTATION *New York to Lisbon**

Both Pan American World Airways and Trans World Airlines have two to four flights a week in season and off season from Idlewild airport. Traveling time is approximately 13 to 14 hours eastbound and approximately 16 hours return. Sleeper berths are available on some flights for $35 a night in addition to regular fare.

Fares—Round Trip

IN SEASON		OFF SEASON	
(April 1–October 31)		(November 1–March 31)	
First Class	$822.30	First Class	$742.30
Tourist Class	$627.90	Tourist Class	$530.90

SEA TRANSPORTATION *New York to Lisbon**

The Italian Lines—operates two very good liners: *Vulcania* and *Saturnia*. There are two sailings a month, and traveling time is approximately eight to ten days.

*Prices and schedules are subject to change at any time. It is advisable to consult your travel agent or write to Casa de Portugal, 630 Fifth Avenue, New York City.

Minimum Fares—Round Trip

IN SEASON		OFF SEASON	
(Eastbound—U.S.A. to Europe: April 12–July 31. Westbound—Europe to U.S.A.: June 28–October 16)		(Eastbound—U.S.A. to Europe: August 1–April 11. Westbound—Europe to U.S.A.: October 17–June 27)	
First	$670	First	$620
Cabin	$580	Cabin	$520
Tourist	$500	Tourist	$400

The Greek Line—operates the *Nea Hellas,* which sails from Lisbon to New York every month. The run from New York to Lisbon is indefinite.

Minimum Fares—Round Trip

IN SEASON		OFF SEASON	
(For dates, see above)		(For dates, see above)	
First	$600	First	$570
Cabin	$500	Cabin	$430
Tourist	$400	Tourist	$360

TRANSPORTATION BETWEEN LISBON AND FÁTIMA*

RAILROAD

Lisbon to Fátima Station			*Bus from Station to Shrine*		
Daily	LV	12:05 P.M.	Daily	LV	3:00 P.M.
	AR	2:44 P.M.		AR	3:50 P.M.
Thursday	LV	8:30 A.M.	Daily	LV	10:25 A.M.
	AR	10:18 A.M.		AR	11:15 A.M.

Bus from Shrine to Station			*Fátima Station to Lisbon*		
Daily	LV	1:25 P.M.	Daily	LV	2:45 P.M.
	AR	2:15 P.M.		AR	5:15 P.M.
Daily	LV	6:40 P.M.	Daily	LV	7:36 P.M.
	AR	7:30 P.M.		AR	11:00 P.M.

PRICE: First Class—70$10 (dollar sign after figure denotes escudos) plus 8$00 for bus fare, a total of 78$10, or $2.75 one way.

NOTE: There is a 20 per cent discount on train fares on the twelfth and thirteenth of May and October. Pilgrims may book tickets directly to the shrine, ensuring a seat on the bus, on ordinary days. On the eleventh, twelfth, and thirteenth of May and October this bus accommodation cannot be guaranteed, but there is a taxi service from the station to the shrine with the approximate cost of $1.50.

BUS DIRECT BETWEEN FÁTIMA AND LISBON

	Lisbon–Fátima		*Fátima–Lisbon*
Daily	LV 9:30 A.M.	Daily	LV 9:50 A.M.
	AR 5:20 P.M.		AR 3:20 P.M.
		Daily	LV 3:30 P.M.
			AR 8:50 P.M.

PRICE: One way—42$60, or $1.50. Agent: Joao Clara, Rua Andrade 16, Lisbon.

TAXI FROM LISBON TO FÁTIMA

Taxis may be hired at the rate of two escudos a kilometer for a car accommodating four persons, or 2$60 per kilometer for a car accommodating six persons. The distance from Lisbon to Fátima and back is 340 kilometers, making a total of 680$00 and 884$00 respectively, or $24.28 and $31.21 round trip, which of course may be shared by the passengers in the car.

*Prices and schedules are subject to change at any time. In Lisbon you may consult for information: George Peabody Associates, Inc., Palacio Foz, Restauradores, Lisbon, Portugal.

Arrangements can be made with the driver for a fixed price before leaving Lisbon.

ACCOMMODATIONS IN FÁTIMA

Any pilgrim may write directly to the Bishop of Leiria, who personally supervises the allotment of rooms in order of application at the sanctuary hospices. These hospices accommodate 300 people in rooms of two, three, or more beds and a few dormitories. There is no fixed charge. The normal offering is about 50$00 or $1.75 per day for food and room for each person.

Reservations may also be made at the following places:

Seminário das Missões, Italian Consolata Fathers.

Accommodations for men at all times, and for married couples during major pilgrimages. For meals and room, 60$00 to 70$00, or $2.10 to $2.45. (This Seminary may be contacted by writing to: John De Marchi, I.M.C., Consolata House of Studies, 5406 Colorado Avenue, N.W., Washington 11, D.C.

Convento das Irmãs Dominicanas, Dominican Sisters.

For men and women, with accommodations for 88 in rooms of one, two, or three and two dormitories, one of six beds, and one of 40 beds. Room with meals from 60$00 to 80$00, or $2.10 to $2.80. Lunch or dinner without room included for 35$00, or $1.23.

Irmãs Concepcionistas, Conception Sisters.

For women only, with accommodations for 50 at about 60$00, or $2.10.

There are three other houses with accommodations for women only, each with room for about 40 pilgrims at the cost of 60$00, or $2.10. They are:

Casa de Nossa Senhora das Dores (Our Lady of Dolors)

Colégio do Sagrado Coração da Maria (Immaculate Heart Sisters)

Irmãs Dorotheias (Dorothean Sisters)

There are also rooms available in the following *pensãos,* but especially for these, reservations must be made well in advance of a pilgrimage.

Pensão de Nossa Senhora do Rosário de Fátima (English proprietress)

Pensão 13 de Maio (English spoken)

Pensão da Sagrada Família

Pensão Católica

Pensão Fátima

At these the rates are 75$00 per person with meals, or $2.63, and 51$00, or $1.80, without meals.

For the pilgrim with a car, who might prefer more comfort, excellent accommodations are to be found at the Estalagem do Cruzeiro at Aljubarrota, half an hour's drive from Fátima. Room with meals per person 90$00, or $3.15. With meals and bath, from 110$00 to 130$00, or $3.85 to $4.55. Room without meals, 50$00, or $1.75. Without meals and with bath, 70$00 to 90$00, or $2.45 to $3.15. Lunch and dinner, 40$00, or $1.40. Breakfast, 12$00, or 45¢.

Appendix Two

FÁTIMA PRAYERS AND DEVOTIONS

THE FIVE FIRST SATURDAYS

The Blessed Virgin Mary appeared to Lucy and said:

"Look, my daughter, my Heart is all pierced with thorns which men drive into it every moment by their blasphemies and ingratitude. Do you at least seek to console me, and let men know that:

"I promise to assist at the hour of death, with the graces necessary for salvation, all those who on the first Saturday of five consecutive months will go to confession, receive Holy Communion, recite the beads, and keep me company during a quarter of an hour, meditating on the fifteen mysteries of the rosary, with the intention of making reparation."

NOTE: Confession may be made eight days before or after that Communion, provided Communion is received in the state of grace. Meditation may bear on one or several mysteries of the rosary.

(*Taken from p. 224, of* Our Lady of Light, *by Barthas and Fonseca, published by Bruce.*)

On June 13, 1912, the Holy Office had already granted a plenary indulgence, under the usual conditions, to those who will accomplish on the first Saturday of any month the special exercises of devotion in honor of the Immaculate Virgin Mary, in reparation for the blasphemies of which her names and prerogatives are the object. Mary's request of Sister Lucy only approves and sanctions a devotion already existing and encouraged by the Church. Those who practice the devotion of the first five Saturdays will thus fulfill the conditions required to gain the plenary indulgence granted by the Holy Office.

THE ANGEL'S PRAYER

My God, I believe, I adore, I hope, and I love You. I beg pardon for those who do not believe, do not adore, do not hope, and do not love You.

Most Holy Trinity, Father, Son, and Holy Ghost, I adore You profoundly, and offer to You the Precious Body, Blood, Soul, and Divinity of Our Lord Jesus Christ, present in all the tabernacles of the world, in reparation for the offenses wherewith You are offended. Through the infinite merits of the Sacred Heart of Jesus and the intercession of the Immaculate Heart of Mary, I plead for the conversion of poor sinners.

OUR LADY'S PRAYERS

On June 13, 1917, the Lady of the Rosary asked the children to say the following prayer after each decade of their rosaries:

"O my Jesus, forgive us. Deliver us from the fire of hell. Bring all souls to heaven, especially those in greatest need."

On July 13, 1917, the Lady of the Rosary said:

"Sacrifice yourselves for sinners; and say often, especially when you make some sacrifice: 'My Jesus, it is for love of You, for the conversion of sinners, and in reparation for sins committed against the Immaculate Heart of Mary.' "

AN ACT OF REPARATION FOR BLASPHEMIES AGAINST THE BLESSED VIRGIN MARY
(*from the Raccolta, New York, Benziger Brothers, Inc.*)

Most glorious Virgin Mary, Mother of God and our Mother, turn thine eyes in pity upon us, miserable sinners; we are sore afflicted by the many evils that surround us in this life, but especially do we feel our hearts break within us upon hearing the dreadful insults and blasphemies uttered against thee, O Virgin Immaculate, to which we are so frequently constrained to listen. O how these impious sayings offend the infinite Majesty of God and of His only-begotten Son, Jesus Christ! How they provoke His indignation and give us cause to fear the terrible effects of His vengeance! Would that the sacrifice of our lives might avail to put an end to such outrages and blasphemies; were it so how gladly we should make it, for we desire, O most holy Mother, to love thee and to honor thee with all our hearts, since this is the will of God. And just because we love thee, we will do all that is in our power to make thee honored and loved by all men. In the meantime do thou our merciful Mother, the supreme comforter of the afflicted, accept this our act of reparation which we offer thee for ourselves and for all our families, as well as for all who impiously blaspheme thee, not knowing what they say. Do thou obtain for them from Almighty God the grace of conversion, and thus render more manifest and more glorious thy kindness, thy power, and thy great mercy.

ACT OF CONSECRATION TO THE IMMACULATE HEART OF MARY

(also from the Raccolta)

O Mary, Virgin most powerful and Mother of Mercy, Queen of Heaven and Refuge of Sinners, we consecrate ourselves to thine Immaculate Heart.

We consecrate to thee our very being and our whole life; all that we have, all that we love, all that we are. To thee we give our bodies, our hearts and our souls; to thee we give our homes, our families, our country. We desire that all that is in us and around us may belong to thee, and may share in the benefits of thy motherly benediction. And that this act of consecration may be truly efficacious and lasting, we renew this day at thy feet the promises of our Baptism and our first Holy Communion. We pledge ourselves to profess courageously and at all times the truths of our holy faith and to live as befits Catholics who are duly submissive to all the directions of the Pope and the Bishops in communion with him. We pledge ourselves to keep the commandments of God and His Church; in particular to keep holy the Lord's Day. We likewise pledge ourselves to make the consoling practices of the Christian religion, and above all, Holy Communion, an integral part of our lives, in so far as we shall be able to do so. Finally, we promise thee, O glorious Mother of God and loving Mother of men, to devote ourselves whole-heartedly to the service of thy blessed cult, in order to hasten and assure, through the sovereignty of thine Immaculate Heart, the coming of the king-

(Indulgence of three years, each time; plenary indulgence under the usual conditions if repeated daily for a month—S.P. Ap., April 29, 1933.)

dom of the Sacred Heart of thine adorable Son in our own hearts and in those of all men, in our country and in all the world, as in heaven, so on earth.

Amen.

PRAYER FOR THE MARIAN YEAR OF 1954

Enraptured by the splendor of your Heavenly beauty and impelled by the anxieties of the world, we cast ourselves into your arms, O Immaculate Mother of Jesus and our Mother, Mary, confident of finding in your most loving heart appeasement of our ardent desires and a safe harbor from the tempests which beset us on every side.

Though degraded by our faults and overwhelmed by infinite misery, we admire and praise the peerless richness of sublime gifts with which God has filled you, above every other mere creature, from the first moment of your Conception until the day after your Assumption into Heaven, He crowned you Queen of the Universe.

O crystal fountain of Faith, bathe our minds with the eternal truths!

O fragrant lily of all holiness, captivate our hearts with your Heavenly perfume!

O conqueress of evil and death, inspire in us a deep horror of sin which makes the soul detestable to God and a slave to hell!

O well-beloved of God: hear the ardent cry which rises up from every heart in this year dedicated to you.

Bend tenderly over our aching wounds. Convert the wicked, dry the tears of the afflicted and oppressed, comfort the poor and humble, quench hatreds, sweeten harshness, safeguard the flower of purity in youth, protect the holy Church, make all men feel the attraction of Christian goodness.

In your name, resounding harmoniously in Heaven, may they recognize that they are brothers, and that the nations are members of one family, upon which may there shine forth the sun of a universal and sincere peace.

Receive, O most sweet Mother, our humble supplications, and above all, obtain for us that one day, happy with you, we may repeat before your throne that hymn which today is sung on earth around your altars:

"You are all beautiful, O Mary! You are the glory, you are the joy, you are the honor of our people! Amen."

—POPE PIUS XII